MULTISENSORY
TEACHING of
Basic Language Skills

ACTIVITY BOOK
Revised Edition

MULTISENSORY
TEACHING of
Basic Language Skills

ACTIVITY BOOK
Revised Edition

by

Suzanne Carreker, Ph.D.

and

Judith R. Birsh, Ed.D.

·P·A·U·L·H·
BROOKES
PUBLISHING CO.®

Baltimore • London • Sydney

Paul H. Brookes Publishing Co.
Post Office Box 10624
Baltimore, Maryland 21285-0624
USA

www.brookespublishing.com

Typeset by Spearhead Global, Inc., Bear, Delaware.
Manufactured in the United States of America by
Victor Graphics, Baltimore, Maryland.

A companion textbook, *Multisensory Teaching of Basic Language Skills, Third Edition* (ISBN-13: 978-1-59857-093-9; ISBN-10: 1-59857-093-5), edited by Judith R. Birsh, is also available from Paul H. Brookes Publishing Co. (1-800-638-3775; 1-410-337-9580).

ISBN-13: 978-1-59857-209-4
ISBN-10: 1-59857-209-1

2015   2014   2013   2012   2011

10   9   8   7   6   5   4   3   2   1

Contents

About the Authors

Suzanne Carreker, Ph.D., is Chief Programs Officer at the Neuhaus Education Center, a nonprofit organization in Houston, Texas, that has offered professional development in evidence-based reading methods to more than 60,000 teachers since its inception in 1980. Dr. Carreker, a past president of the Houston Branch of The International Dyslexia Association (HBIDA) and a current vice president of the national IDA board, is a frequent speaker at regional and national conferences and has authored a number of multisensory curricula and journal articles. She was the recipient of the 2009 HBIDA Nancy LaFevers Award for her contributions to students with dyslexia and other related learning differences in the Houston community.

Judith R. Birsh, Ed.D., has an enduring belief that well-prepared, informed teachers are the major influence on effective instruction in the field of reading and dyslexia. This belief had its beginning in 1960 when she met her first student who, although 18 years old, read poorly. The quest to find answers to this puzzle led her to a master's degree in remedial reading and a doctorate in reading and language at Teachers College, Columbia University. After training with Aylett R. Cox in Dallas, Texas she became a Certified Academic Language Therapist and Qualified Instructor, founding and directing the Multisensory Teaching of Basic Language Skills courses at Teachers College in the Department of Curriculum and Teaching, Program in Learning Disabilities. After her retirement in 2000, Dr. Birsh has maintained her commitment to teacher preparation, giving professional development workshops, consulting with private and public schools, writing articles, and working with students with dyslexia. In 2008 she received the Luke Waites Academic Language Therapy Association Award of Service and the Margaret Byrd Rawson Lifetime Achievement Award from the International Dyslexia Association.

Introduction

The purpose of the revised edition of the *Multisensory Teaching of Basic Language Skills Activity Book* is to help reinforce the information gained during teacher preparation from texts, classroom lectures, and practicums. These opportunities to reflect on and assimilate newly acquired linguistic concepts provide teachers with a check of their knowledge and practice skills. In addition, the activities can act as a platform from which to plan lessons with these concepts for their students.

Teacher knowledge is essential to student success (Brady & Moats, 1997; Piasta, Connor, Fishman, & Morrison, 2009). Teachers must understand the theoretical underpinnings of literacy acquisition. They must know effective methods for teaching literacy skills and how to differentiate their instruction to meet the needs of all students. Teachers themselves must possess underlying linguistic skills and insights about different language structures so that they can successfully instruct their students. The textbook *Multisensory Teaching of Basic Language Skills, Third Edition* (Birsh, 2011) provides teachers with current research findings and specific multisensory methods of instruction in all areas of literacy. This activity book is a supplement to that textbook and contains activities that reinforce and extend the information presented in it. The activities are designed to target and refine necessary linguistic skills and insights about language structures that teachers need. In addition, the activities are also coordinated with Chapters 3–8 of the textbook *Becoming a Professional Reading Teacher* (Aaron, Joshi, & Quatroche, 2008).

The matrix on the following pages coordinates the activities in the workbook with the chapters in the Birsh (2011) textbook. As chapters in that textbook are read, activities that relate to the chapters can be completed, or the exercises in this activity book can be completed in order and then related chapters in the textbook can be read and referenced. An icon appearing at the top right corner of an activity indicates the chapter(s) from the textbook that would be particularly helpful for users to refer to while completing the activity. Referrals to a teacher web site following some activities offer readers demonstrations of teachers engaged in teaching those concepts.

All of the activities are designed to enhance the knowledge base of teachers. Some of the activities can be adapted for use with students. For example, interspersed among the activities are 21 Try This exercises that are designed specifically for use with students in the classroom or small-group settings. Furthermore, Appendixes A–P contain many resources teachers can use to enhance their own understanding of linguistic concepts and their presentation to their students. There are reproducible games, charts, graphic organizers, word lists, comprehension passages, and templates for lesson plans. There is an Answer Key for all of the activities so that teachers can check their understanding while they are learning new skills. A guide to activities coordinated with the Aaron et al. (2008) textbook can be found following the Answer Key.

NOTE TO MULTISENSORY STRUCTURED LANGUAGE EDUCATION TEACHER EDUCATORS

Some of the activities in the workbook share the same title. For example, Activities 13 and 14 are both titled *Phoneme Checklist*. In a training setting, participants complete the first activity for practice. The second activity with the same title could be completed as an assessment.

REFERENCES

Aaron, P.G., Joshi, R.M., & Quatroche, D. (2008). *Becoming a professional reading teacher.* Baltimore: Paul H. Brookes Publishing Co.

Birsh, J.R. (Ed.). (2011). *Multisensory teaching of basic language skills* (3rd ed.). Baltimore: Paul H. Brookes Publishing Co.

Brady, S., & Moats, L.C. (1997). *Informed instruction for reading success: Foundations for teacher preparation* (A position paper of The International Dyslexia Association). Baltimore: The International Dyslexia Association.

Piasta, S.B., Connor, C.M., Fishman, B.J., & Morrison, F.J. (2009). Teachers' knowledge of literary concepts, classroom practices, and student reading growth. *Scientific Studies of Reading, 13*(3), 224–248.

Activity–Chapter Matrix

	Chapter 1	Chapter 2	Chapter 3	Chapter 4	Chapter 5	Chapter 6	Chapter 7	Chapter 8	Chapter 9	Chapter 10	Chapter 11	Chapter 12	Chapter 13	Chapter 14	Chapter 15	Chapter 16	Chapter 17	Chapter 18	Chapter 19	Chapter 20	Chapter 21	Chapter 22	Chapter 23
Activity 1	✓	✓																					
Activity 2	✓	✓																					
Activity 3			✓																				
Activity 4			✓					✓	✓														
Activity 5				✓				✓	✓														
Activity 6				✓				✓	✓							✓							
Try This 1				✓				✓	✓							✓							
Activity 7				✓				✓	✓							✓							
Try This 2				✓				✓	✓							✓							
Activity 8					✓			✓	✓							✓							
Activity 9					✓			✓	✓							✓							
Activity 10					✓			✓	✓							✓							
Activity 11					✓			✓	✓							✓							
Activity 12					✓			✓	✓							✓							
Activity 13					✓			✓	✓							✓							
Activity 14					✓			✓	✓							✓							
Activity 15					✓			✓	✓							✓							
Activity 16					✓			✓	✓														
Activity 17					✓			✓	✓							✓							
Activity 18					✓			✓	✓							✓							
Activity 19					✓			✓	✓							✓							
Activity 20					✓			✓	✓							✓							
Activity 21					✓	✓		✓	✓														
Activity 22					✓	✓		✓	✓														
Activity 23						✓																	
Try This 3						✓																	
Activity 24						✓																	
Activity 25						✓																	
Try This 4						✓																	
Activity 26					✓	✓																	
Activity 27				✓	✓	✓																	
Activity 28							✓																
Activity 29							✓																
Activity 30							✓																
Activity 31							✓																
Activity 32							✓								✓								
Activity 33								✓								✓							
Activity 34								✓								✓							
Activity 35								✓								✓							
Activity 36								✓								✓							
Activity 37								✓								✓							
Activity 38								✓								✓							

	Chapter 1	Chapter 2	Chapter 3	Chapter 4	Chapter 5	Chapter 6	Chapter 7	Chapter 8	Chapter 9	Chapter 10	Chapter 11	Chapter 12	Chapter 13	Chapter 14	Chapter 15	Chapter 16	Chapter 17	Chapter 18	Chapter 19	Chapter 20	Chapter 21	Chapter 22	Chapter 23
Activity 39								✓								✓							
Activity 40								✓								✓							
Activity 41					✓	✓		✓								✓							
Activity 42								✓								✓							
Activity 43								✓								✓							
Activity 44								✓								✓							
Activity 45								✓								✓							
Activity 46								✓								✓							
Activity 47								✓								✓							
Try This 5a & 5b								✓								✓							
Activity 48								✓								✓							
Try This 6								✓								✓							
Activity 49								✓								✓							
Try This 7								✓								✓							
Activity 50								✓								✓							
Activity 51								✓								✓							
Activity 52								✓								✓							
Activity 53								✓								✓							
Activity 54								✓								✓							
Try This 8								✓								✓							
Activity 55								✓								✓							
Activity 56								✓								✓							
Activity 57								✓			✓					✓							
Activity 58								✓			✓					✓							
Activity 59								✓			✓					✓							
Activity 60								✓			✓					✓							
Activity 61								✓															
Activity 62								✓															
Try This 9								✓															
Activity 63								✓															
Activity 64								✓		✓													
Activity 65								✓		✓													
Activity 66								✓		✓													
Try This 10								✓															
Activity 67									✓														
Activity 68									✓														
Activity 69									✓														
Activity 70									✓														
Activity 71									✓														
Activity 72									✓														
Try This 11									✓														
Activity 73									✓														
Activity 74									✓														

	Chapter 1	Chapter 2	Chapter 3	Chapter 4	Chapter 5	Chapter 6	Chapter 7	Chapter 8	Chapter 9	Chapter 10	Chapter 11	Chapter 12	Chapter 13	Chapter 14	Chapter 15	Chapter 16	Chapter 17	Chapter 18	Chapter 19	Chapter 20	Chapter 21	Chapter 22	Chapter 23
Activity 75									✓														
Activity 76									✓														
Activity 77								✓			✓					✓							
Activity 78								✓			✓					✓							
Activity 79								✓			✓					✓							
Activity 80								✓			✓					✓							
Try This 12								✓			✓					✓							
Activity 81											✓												
Activity 82											✓												
Activity 83											✓												
Try This 13											✓												
Try This 14											✓												
Try This 15											✓												
Activity 84											✓												
Try This 16											✓												
Activity 85											✓												
Activity 86											✓												
Try This 17											✓												
Activity 87											✓												
Activity 88											✓												
Activity 89											✓	✓											
Activity 90												✓											
Activity 91												✓											
Try This 18												✓											
Activity 92												✓											
Try This 19												✓											
Activity 93													✓										
Activity 94													✓										
Activity 95													✓										
Activity 96													✓										
Try This 20													✓										
Activity 97													✓										
Activity 98													✓										
Activity 99													✓										
Activity 100									✓							✓							
Activity 101														✓									
Activity 102															✓								
Activity 103																			✓				
Activity 104																				✓			
Activity 105																	✓	✓			✓	✓	
Try This 21																					✓		

ACTIVITY 1
Terms for Research and Multisensory Teaching

Match each term with the correct definition. Use Chapters 1 and 2 in *Multisensory Teaching of Basic Language Skills, Third Edition* (Birsh, 2011) for reference.

1. _____ qualitative research
2. _____ quantitative research
3. _____ experimental research
4. _____ quasi-experimental research
5. _____ metacognition
6. _____ left temporal cortex
7. _____ left frontal cortex
8. _____ occipital cortex
9. _____ auditory
10. _____ visual
11. _____ modality
12. _____ kinesthetic
13. _____ multisensory
14. _____ tactile
15. _____ word blindness
16. _____ angular gyrus
17. _____ dyslexia

a. Area of the brain for language comprehension
b. Related to muscle movement and memory
c. Early term for dyslexia
d. Area of the brain for speech production
e. A specific sensory pathway
f. Related to touch
g. Area of the brain for visual processing
h. Related to seeing
i. Pertaining to the simultaneous use of multiple senses
j. Area of brain for visual–verbal associations
k. Research in which the subjects are randomly assigned to experimental and control groups
l. Deliberate rearrangement of information
m. Research conducted without randomized assignment of subjects to experimental and control groups
n. Related to hearing
o. A specific language-based disorder characterized by difficulty with single-word reading
p. Research in which results are based on a large sample that is representative of the population
q. Research that collects data through various kinds of observations

Appendix A on pages 133–134 summarizes the major findings of recent research and may be photocopied for informational purposes and distributed to educators, administrators, and parents.

The Brain

Multiple sites in the brain are activated when a student reads. The different sites perform specific functions during reading and rely on connections with other sites. Research has shown that there are neural abnormalities in the language areas of the left hemisphere in a student with a language-based reading disability (Farrell & Sherman, 2011; Rumsey, 1996).

Use Figure 1 to label the various parts of the brain and their function in terms of reading. Use Chapters 1 and 2 of Birsh (2011) for reference.

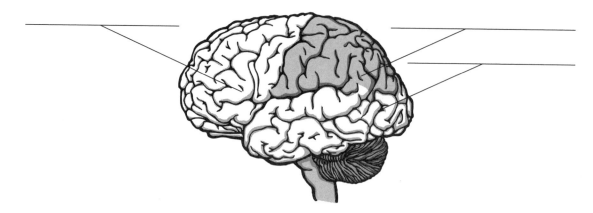

Figure 1.   The brain's four cortical lobes. (From Kaufman C. [2011] *Executive function in the classroom* [p. 27]. Baltimore: Paul H. Brookes Publishing Co.; reprinted by permission.)

Terms for Oral Language

Match each term with the correct definition. Use Chapter 3 in Birsh (2011) for reference.

1. _____ metalinguistics
2. _____ aspiration
3. _____ suprasegmentals
4. _____ pragmatics
5. _____ affixes
6. _____ dyspraxia
7. _____ phonology, morphology, syntax
8. _____ dysarthria
9. _____ schwa
10. _____ semantics

a. Speech problems caused by sensorimotor disruption
b. The melody of speech—stress, pitch, loudness, and so forth
c. The sound /ə/
d. Content of language
e. Puff of air
f. Awareness of language as an entity
g. Use of language
h. Prefixes and suffixes
i. Speech problems caused by musculature weaknesses
j. Domains of language

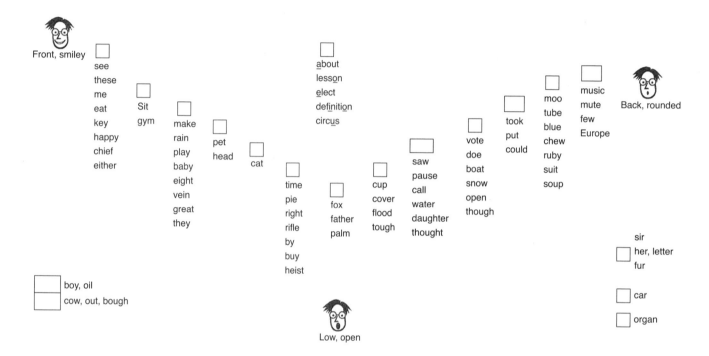

Phonemes

Vowels

TEXTBOOK REFERENCE
Chapters 3, 8, and 9

Vowels sounds are created with positions of the jaw, tongue, and lips (Moats, 1995, 2000; Soifer, 2011). The jaw opens to varying degrees. The tongue may be front or back and high or low. The lips may be rounded or not rounded. The awareness of the speech features helps with the pronunciation and identification of speech sounds. Fill in the missing vowels in Figure 2, the Vowel Chart. Notice the positions of your jaw, tongue, and lips as you say each vowel sound. Use Chapter 3 in Birsh (2011) for reference.

Figure 2. Vowel Chart. (From Moats, LC. [2010]. *Speech to print: Language essentials for teachers* [2nd ed. p. 96]. Baltimore: Paul H. Brookes Publishing Co.; adapted by permission.)

Clues for Identifying Word Origin

The Anglo-Saxon, Latin, and Greek languages greatly influenced written English. Students who understand the history of English have additional strategies for reading and spelling unfamiliar words (Henry, 1988, 2010). Identify the language layer that is characterized by the following letter patterns or word structures. Write *Anglo-Saxon*, *Latin*, or *Greek*. Use Chapter 4 in Birsh (2011) for reference.

1. The consonant pairs *gn, kn,* and *wr*   _____

2. Roots that end in *ct* and *pt*   _____

3. Vowel pairs   _____

4. Initial consonant clusters *rh, pt, pn,* and *ps*   _____

5. Chameleon prefixes   _____

6. Common, everyday words   _____

7. The consonant cluster *ch* pronounced /k/   _____

8. The letters *c, s,* and *t* pronounced /sh/   _____

9. Medial *y*   _____

10. Consonant digraphs *ch, sh, th,* and *wh*   _____

11. The affixing of roots   _____

12. Compound words   _____

13. Combining forms   _____

14. The affixing of base words   _____

15. The consonant cluster *ph* pronounced /f/   _____

16. The schwa or unstressed vowel sound   _____

Identifying Word Origin

Identify the origin—Anglo-Saxon, Latin, or Greek—of the following words. Use the clues from the previous activity and Chapter 4 in Birsh (2011) for reference.

1. scholar _____
2. dislike _____
3. that _____
4. construction _____
5. phonograph _____
6. made _____
7. excellent _____
8. boat _____
9. conductor _____
10. barn _____
11. microscope _____
12. direction _____
13. transport _____
14. symphony _____
15. chloroplast _____

16. hardware _____
17. photograph _____
18. shipyard _____
19. respect _____
20. spatial _____
21. water _____
22. manuscript _____
23. timely _____
24. portable _____
25. heart _____
26. good _____
27. introduction _____
28. transcript _____
29. bread _____
30. bad _____

TRY THIS

1 Sorting Words by Origin

1. Write words of Anglo-Saxon, Latin, and Greek origin on separate cards.
2. Have students sort words into three piles based on origin: Anglo-Saxon, Latin, or Greek.

Identifying Word Origin

Identify the origin—Anglo-Saxon, Latin, or Greek—of the following words. Use the clues from Activity 5 and Chapter 4 in Birsh (2011) for reference.

1. food _____
2. rhythm _____
3. lotion _____
4. reject _____
5. eruption _____
6. chorus _____
7. thermometer _____
8. gather _____
9. induction _____
10. intersect _____

11. psychology _____
12. rhododendron _____
13. helpless _____
14. napkin _____
15. wait _____
16. destruction _____
17. sympathy _____
18. football _____
19. illegal _____
20. conduct _____

TRY THIS

2 Word Origin Concentration Game

1. Create a concentration game board using the template on page 137.
2. Prepare the game board as an overhead transparency or an interactive whiteboard.
3. Choose two words each of Anglo-Saxon, Latin, and Greek origin (six words total).
4. Write these words randomly in the empty spaces on the game board.
5. Write the languages of origin that represent the six words randomly in the remaining spaces.
6. Cover each of the spaces with small sticky notes.
7. Place the transparency on the overhead projector.
8. Divide students into teams and determine a rotation.
9. Teams take turns calling out pairs of coordinates (e.g., A3 and B3) to search for a word and an origin that match.
10. Uncover the spaces that correspond to the coordinates.
11. If the word and origin match, the team gets a point.
12. If the word and origin do not match, cover the two spaces again with the sticky notes.
13. Each team gets only one turn per round, regardless of whether the team has scored a point.
14. The game continues until all of the squares have been uncovered.

Consonant Phonemes
Place of Articulation

When students are aware of the visual display and kinesthetic feel of phonemes, they can identify phonemes in a word and clarify phonemes that are similar (Carreker, 2011a; Moats 1995, 2000; Soifer, 2011). The place of articulation is the place where the flow of air is blocked or changed during production of a consonant sound. Write the following consonant sounds in the appropriate column according to the place of articulation.

/b/   /d/   /ch/   /f/   /g/   /h/   /j/   /k/   /l/   /m/   /n/   /ng/

/p/   /r/   /s/   /sh/   /t/   /th/   /th/   /v/   /w/   /y/   /z/   /zh/

Both lips	Teeth and lower lip	Between the teeth	Ridge behind the teeth	Roof of the mouth	Back of the mouth	From the throat

Consonant Phonemes
Blocked, Partially Blocked, and Unblocked

TEXTBOOK REFERENCE
Chapters 5, 8, 9, and 16

The terms *blocked*, *partially blocked*, and *unblocked* are used in decoding and spelling instruction to refer to the kinesthetic feel of the position of the tongue, teeth, and lips during the production sounds in isolation (Carreker, 2011a, 2011b). In decoding instruction, *blocked* refers to the steady position of the tongue, teeth, or lips during the entire production of a sound. *Partially blocked* refers to a released position of the tongue or lips during the production of a sound. *Unblocked* refers to no obstruction of the sound by the tongue, teeth, or lips during the production of sounds. These terms are used to aid students in clearly feeling and distinguishing sound.

Sort the consonant sounds below as *blocked*, *partially blocked*, or *unblocked*.

/b/   /d/   /ch/   /f/   /g/   /h/   /j/   /k/   /l/   /m/   /n/   /ng/

/p/   /r/   /s/   /sh/   /t/   /th/   /th/   /v/   /w/   /y/   /z/   /zh/

Blocked	Partially blocked	Unblocked

Phonemes
Voiced and Unvoiced Consonants

Some sounds activate the vocal cords during production. These sounds are referred to as *voiced*. Some sounds do not activate the vocal cords during production. These sounds are referred to as *unvoiced*. Write the following consonant sounds in the appropriate column.

/b/   /d/   /ch/   /f/   /g/   /h/   /j/   /k/   /l/   /m/   /n/   /ng/

/p/   /r/   /s/   /sh/   /t/   /th/   /<u>th</u>/   /v/   /w/   /y/   /z/   /zh/

Voiced	Unvoiced

Consonant Phonemes
Cognates

Cognate phonemes have the same visual display, mouth position, and place of articulation (Carreker, 2011b). The only difference is that one sound activates the vocal cords (voiced) and one does not (unvoiced). For example, /ch/ and /j/ are cognates. When you produce these sounds, the visual display, mouth position, and place of articulation are the same. The difference is that your vocal cords are activated when you produce /j/ as in *jeep* (a voiced phoneme) and are not activated when you produce /ch/ as in *cheep* (an unvoiced phoneme). Write the cognates to each phoneme.

Unvoiced	Voiced
/ch/	/j/
/t/	
/f/	
/k/	
/p/	
/s/	
/sh/	
/th/	

Consonant Phonemes
Continuant and Clipped

TEXTBOOK REFERENCE
Chapters 5, 8, 9, and 16

Some consonant sounds are *continuants* and are prolonged in their production, such as /m/ and /n/. Some consonant sounds are *stop sounds* and are obstructed at the place of articulation and are not prolonged in their production, such as /t/ and /p/. During classroom instruction, it is important to clip these stop consonant sounds to prevent the addition of the /uh/ at the end of the sound. These stop sounds are also referred to as *clipped* sounds (Carreker, 2011b). Look at these consonant sounds and determine if in their production they are continuant or clipped. Write *continuant* or *clipped* to the right of each sound.

1. /t/ _____

2. /m/ _____

3. /p/ _____

4. /n/ _____

5. /s/ _____

6. /l/ _____

7. /j/ _____

8. /b/ _____

9. /g/ _____

10. /v/ _____

11. /y/ _____

12. /r/ _____

13. /z/ _____

14. /d/ _____

Phoneme Checklist

TEXTBOOK REFERENCE
Chapters 5, 8, 9, and 16

This checklist incorporates all the information about sounds from the previous six activities. Thorough understanding of the look and feel of sounds aids correct sound production. For example, /m/ is blocked, voiced, and a continuant, and /p/ is partially blocked, unvoiced, and clipped.

/l/ as in *leaf*
- ❑ open
- ❑ voiced
- ❑ continuant
- ❑ partially blocked
- ❑ unvoiced
- ❑ clipped
- ❑ blocked

d/ as in *dog*
- ❑ open
- ❑ voiced
- ❑ continuant
- ❑ partially blocked
- ❑ unvoiced
- ❑ clipped
- ❑ blocked

/g/ as in *goat*
- ❑ open
- ❑ voiced
- ❑ continuant
- ❑ partially blocked
- ❑ unvoiced
- ❑ clipped
- ❑ blocked

/b/ as in *bat*
- ❑ open
- ❑ voiced
- ❑ continuant
- ❑ partially blocked
- ❑ unvoiced
- ❑ clipped
- ❑ blocked

/th/ as in thin
- ❑ open
- ❑ voiced
- ❑ continuant
- ❑ partially blocked
- ❑ unvoiced
- ❑ clipped
- ❑ blocked

/ch/ as in *chin*
- ❑ open
- ❑ voiced
- ❑ continuant
- ❑ partially blocked
- ❑ unvoiced
- ❑ clipped
- ❑ blocked

/w/ as in *wagon*
- ❑ open
- ❑ voiced
- ❑ continuant
- ❑ partially blocked
- ❑ unvoiced
- ❑ clipped
- ❑ blocked

/h/ as in *house*
- ❑ open
- ❑ voiced
- ❑ partially blocked
- ❑ unvoiced
- ❑ blocked

/m/ as in *mitten*
- ❑ open
- ❑ voiced
- ❑ continuant
- ❑ partially blocked
- ❑ unvoiced
- ❑ clipped
- ❑ blocked

/j/ as in *jump*
- ❑ open
- ❑ voiced
- ❑ continuant
- ❑ partially blocked
- ❑ unvoiced
- ❑ clipped
- ❑ blocked

/zh/ as in *erosion*
- ❑ open
- ❑ voiced
- ❑ continuant
- ❑ partially blocked
- ❑ unvoiced
- ❑ clipped
- ❑ blocked

/s/ as in *sock*
- ❑ open
- ❑ voiced
- ❑ continuant
- ❑ partially blocked
- ❑ unvoiced
- ❑ clipped
- ❑ blocked

Phoneme Checklist

Check that appropriate descriptions for each phoneme listed below.

/y/ as in *yellow*
- ❑ open
- ❑ voiced
- ❑ continuant
- ❑ partially blocked
- ❑ unvoiced
- ❑ clipped
- ❑ blocked

/z/ as in *zipper*
- ❑ open
- ❑ voiced
- ❑ continuant
- ❑ partially blocked
- ❑ unvoiced
- ❑ clipped
- ❑ blocked

/n/ as in *nest*
- ❑ open
- ❑ voiced
- ❑ continuant
- ❑ partially blocked
- ❑ unvoiced
- ❑ clipped
- ❑ blocked

/ng/ as in *sink*
- ❑ open
- ❑ voiced
- ❑ continuant
- ❑ partially blocked
- ❑ unvoiced
- ❑ clipped
- ❑ blocked

/k/ as in *kite*
- ❑ open
- ❑ voiced
- ❑ continuant
- ❑ partially blocked
- ❑ unvoiced
- ❑ clipped
- ❑ blocked

/p/ as in *pig*
- ❑ open
- ❑ voiced
- ❑ continuant
- ❑ partially blocked
- ❑ unvoiced
- ❑ clipped
- ❑ blocked

/sh/ as in *ship*
- ❑ open
- ❑ voiced
- ❑ continuant
- ❑ partially blocked
- ❑ unvoiced
- ❑ clipped
- ❑ blocked

/t/ as in *table*
- ❑ open
- ❑ voiced
- ❑ continuant
- ❑ partially blocked
- ❑ unvoiced
- ❑ clipped
- ❑ blocked

/f/ as in *fish*
- ❑ open
- ❑ voiced
- ❑ continuant
- ❑ partially blocked
- ❑ unvoiced
- ❑ clipped
- ❑ blocked

/th/ as in *mother*
- ❑ open
- ❑ voiced
- ❑ continuant
- ❑ partially blocked
- ❑ unvoiced
- ❑ clipped
- ❑ blocked

/v/ as in *valentine*
- ❑ open
- ❑ voiced
- ❑ continuant
- ❑ partially blocked
- ❑ unvoiced
- ❑ clipped
- ❑ blocked

/r/ as in *rabbit*
- ❑ open
- ❑ voiced
- ❑ continuant
- ❑ partially blocked
- ❑ unvoiced
- ❑ clipped
- ❑ blocked

Classification of Phonemes

Match the terms with the appropriate definition.

1. _____ nasal

2. _____ stop

3. _____ fricative

4. _____ affricate

5. _____ glide

6. _____ liquid

a. A consonant sound that consists of a slowly released stop followed by a fricative
b. A sound produced by forcing air through the nose
c. A sound that produces by forcing air through a narrow opening between the teeth and lips to make a hissing sound
d. A sound produced when the lips and/or tongue are passing from the position for one sound to that of another
e. A sound in which the outgoing air flow is completely stopped
f. Flowing and vowellike

Match the sounds with their classification.

7. _____ /t/, /k/

8. _____ /n/, /m/

9. _____ /f/, /z/

10. _____ /ch/, /j/

11. _____ /w/, /y/

12. _____ /l/, /r/

g. nasals

h. affricates

i. stops

j. fricatives

k. liquids

l. glides

Phonemic Awareness Activities

Phonological awareness is a broad term that describes the sound structure of language. Phonological awareness skills develop hierarchically from rhyming to syllable counting to detecting and manipulating phonemes (Uhry, 2011). Activities that specifically deal with phonemes in words are referred to as *phonemic awareness activities*. Sort the following phonemic awareness activities by type. Place the number of the activity in the correct column.

1. What word is /m/.../ă/.../t/?
2. Change the /l/ in *lip* to /s/.
3. What sounds are in *mat*?
4. What word does not belong: *make, miss, tip*?
5. What is *stop* without /s/?
6. What is the medial sound of *cat*?
7. How many sounds are in *cheek*?
8. What is the first sound in *lamp*?
9. Add /s/ to the beginning of *lip*.
10. Which word has three sounds: *ship* or *last*?
11. What is the final sound in *pig*?
12. What word is /c/.../l/.../ŏ/.../k/?

Isolation/identification	Blending	Segmentation	Deletion/addition

How Many Phonemes?

A phoneme is the smallest unit of sound that distinguishes one word from another. A beginning reader's ability to segment a word into its constituent phonemes is one of the best predictors of reading success. How many phonemes are represented in each word?

1. mat _____
2. cash _____
3. ship _____
4. match _____
5. stop _____
6. knife _____
7. scratch _____
8. truck _____
9. love _____
10. spell _____

11. stand _____
12. child _____
13. month _____
14. think _____
15. peach _____
16. queen _____
17. train _____
18. climb _____
19. strike _____
20. blank _____

How Many Phonemes?

How many phonemes are represented in each word?

1. show _____

2. splint _____

3. knee _____

4. badge _____

5. past _____

6. face _____

7. thrill _____

8. clock _____

9. give _____

10. shack _____

11. strand _____

12. teeth _____

13. church _____

14. shrink _____

15. enough _____

16. quit _____

17. fix _____

18. smile _____

19. night _____

20. flax _____

Same Phoneme?

The same phoneme can be represented with different graphemes. The same grapheme can represent more than one phoneme. There are variations of some phonemes that can be represented by the same grapheme. These variants are called allophones and are not separate phonemes. For example, the phoneme represented by initial *p* in the word *pop* is a slight variation of the phoneme represented by final *p*. the initial phoneme is aspirated as /pʰ/. The final phoneme is /p/. Look at the underlined graphemes in each pair of words below. Do the underlined graphemes in each pair represent the same phoneme, do they represent different phonemes, or is one of the phonemes an allophone? If the underlined graphemes represent the same phoneme, write *yes* beside each pair. If the underlined graphemes represent different phonemes or if one of the phonemes is an allophone, write *no* beside each pair.

		Same?				Same?
1.	s<u>ai</u>d	b<u>e</u>d	_____	11.	ar<u>ch</u>	e<u>ch</u>o	_____
2.	spin<u>s</u>	spin<u>s</u>	_____	12.	<u>s</u>plint	jump<u>ed</u>	_____
3.	ba<u>th</u>	sa<u>f</u>e	_____	13.	si<u>n</u>k	si<u>n</u>g	_____
4.	st<u>ea</u>k	v<u>ei</u>n	_____	14.	f<u>ir</u>st	f<u>er</u>n	_____
5.	ni<u>gh</u>t	t<u>ie</u>	_____	15.	ten<u>s</u>e	fa<u>c</u>e	_____
6.	m<u>a</u>rket	m<u>u</u>stard	_____	16.	fl<u>y</u>	penn<u>y</u>	_____
7.	<u>th</u>at	<u>v</u>ase	_____	17.	rhy<u>th</u>m	rhy<u>m</u>e	_____
8.	p<u>ea</u>ch	pr<u>ie</u>st	_____	18.	<u>z</u>ipper	pan<u>s</u>y	_____
9.	pl<u>ai</u>d	bl<u>a</u>st	_____	19.	gra<u>f</u>t	gra<u>ph</u>	_____
10.	<u>o</u>rbit	act<u>or</u>	_____	20.	land<u>ed</u>	seem<u>ed</u>	_____

Look at the underlined graphemes in each pair of words. If the underlined graphemes represent the same phoneme, write *yes* beside each pair. If the underlined graphemes represent different phonemes or if one of the phonemes is an allophone, write *no* beside each pair.

		Same?					Same?
1.	v<u>ie</u>w	sh<u>oe</u>	_____	11.	<u>th</u>at	wi<u>th</u>	_____
2.	w<u>a</u>sh	m<u>a</u>sh	_____	12.	si<u>n</u>gle	fi<u>n</u>ger	_____
3.	<u>t</u>ent	ten<u>t</u>	_____	13.	<u>j</u>eep	<u>g</u>irl	_____
4.	b<u>oy</u>	b<u>oi</u>l	_____	14.	r<u>aw</u>	h<u>au</u>l	_____
5.	can<u>y</u>on	<u>y</u>ellow	_____	15.	<u>g</u>em	<u>j</u>et	_____
6.	doc<u>t</u>or	shor<u>t</u>age	_____	16.	w<u>a</u>ter	p<u>o</u>lish	_____
7.	<u>sh</u>ack	wa<u>sh</u>	_____	17.	hea<u>l</u>	hea<u>l</u>th	_____
8.	<u>i</u>sle	sp<u>y</u>	_____	18.	gr<u>ou</u>p	gr<u>ou</u>t	_____
9.	r<u>oo</u>m	fr<u>ui</u>t	_____	19.	tr<u>oo</u>p	s<u>ou</u>p	_____
10.	bal<u>le</u>t	surv<u>ey</u>	_____	20.	ga<u>s</u>	hi<u>s</u>	_____

How Many Letters and How Many Phonemes?

The number of letters and the number of phonemes in a word may differ. Write the number of letters and the number of phonemes for each word.

		Letters	Phonemes
1.	broom	_____	_____
2.	knee	_____	_____
3.	shrimp	_____	_____
4.	splint	_____	_____
5.	sprint	_____	_____
6.	lead	_____	_____
7.	grasp	_____	_____
8.	sound	_____	_____
9.	blame	_____	_____
10.	sing	_____	_____

		Letters	Phonemes
11.	mix	_____	_____
12.	show	_____	_____
13.	left	_____	_____
14.	child	_____	_____
15.	space	_____	_____
16.	teach	_____	_____
17.	both	_____	_____
18.	spend	_____	_____
19.	kind	_____	_____
20.	knowledge	_____	_____

ACTIVITY 22

How Many Letters and
How Many Phonemes?

TEXTBOOK REFERENCE
Chapters 5, 6, 8, and 9

Write the number of letters and the number of phonemes for each word.

		Letters	Phonemes				Letters	Phonemes
1.	judge	_____	_____		11.	most	_____	_____
2.	need	_____	_____		12.	shout	_____	_____
3.	peach	_____	_____		13.	shrill	_____	_____
4.	thrill	_____	_____		14.	less	_____	_____
5.	know	_____	_____		15.	close	_____	_____
6.	plan	_____	_____		16.	cloth	_____	_____
7.	clasp	_____	_____		17.	splice	_____	_____
8.	knife	_____	_____		18.	trend	_____	_____
9.	may	_____	_____		19.	jacket	_____	_____
10.	stray	_____	_____		20.	muskrat	_____	_____

Letter Shapes and Names

Calling attention to how letters look aids students in their ability to instantly recognize letters. Printed letters are composed of all straight lines, all curved lines, or a combination of straight and curved lines. Write each uppercase or capital letter of the alphabet in the column that best describes the letter. Do the same with the lowercase printed letters.

All straight lines	All curved lines	Straight and curved lines
A	C	B

TRY THIS

3   Instant Letter Recognition

1. Make a photocopy of the Instant Letter Recognition Chart on page 135.
2. Fill the chart with six letters that repeat in a different order in each row.
3. Prepare the chart as an overhead transparency or on an interactive whiteboard.
4. Touch and name the letters in the first row.
5. Touch the letters in the first row as students name them.
6. Start again at the top. Touch the letters as quickly possible, working across each row and down the chart, row by row.
7. Time the students for 1 minute.
8. The initial goal is for students to read the chart two times in 1 minute. The goal for students in grades 3 and higher is to read the chart four times in 1 minute.

From Carreker, S. (2011b). Teaching reading: Accurate decoding. In J.R. Birsh (Ed.), *Multisensory teaching of basic language skills* (3rd ed., p. 207). Baltimore: Paul H. Brookes Publishing Co.; adapted by permission.

Quartiles for Dictionary Work

The alphabet can be divided into quartiles that roughly match the division of a dictionary into four equal sections. Knowledge of quartiles enables students to open the dictionary in close proximity to where a word may be found instead of having to begin at the front of the dictionary and turn every page. The letters that begin the four quartiles are *A, E, M,* and *S*. A mnemonic sentence such as *All Eagles Must Soar* aids the memory of the quartiles (Allen, 2011).

Write the letters that are part of each quartile.

First quartile	A	_____
Second quartile	E	_____
Third quartile	M	_____
Fourth quartile	S	_____

In which quartile is each letter found—first, second, third, or fourth?

L _____   S _____

C _____   J _____

X _____   L _____

O _____   I _____

B _____   Q _____

In which quartile is each word found—first, second, third, or fourth?

graph _____   never _____

review _____   compare _____

which _____   model _____

develop _____   theme _____

kangaroo _____   pumpkin _____

Carreker and Birsh

Guide Words for Dictionary Work

Guide words are found at the top of a dictionary page and are used to determine whether a target word is on that page. The guide word on the left represents the first entry word on the page. The guide word on the right represents the last entry word on the page. A target word must fall after the left guide word and before the guide word on the right to be located on the page. If the target word is on the page and before the first entry word in the second column of the page, it is located in the first column (Allen, 2011). Look at the following diagram, which shows two guide words on a dictionary page (*juncture* and *juvenile*) and the word that appears at the top of the second column (*jurisdiction*). In the list of target words below the diagram, first determine whether each target word falls on the page, before the page, or after the page. If the target word falls on the page, determine whether it falls in the first or the second column.

juncture	juvenile
	jurisdiction

	On the page	Before the page	After the page	First column	Second column
jump					
justice					
juxtaposition					
judicial					
jungle					
junket					
July					
juxtapose					
juice					
jury					

TRY THIS

4   Dictionary Relay

1. Make a photocopy of the Dictionary Relay chart on page 136.
2. Fill the chart with 15 target words and make appropriate number of photocopies.
3. Students work in teams of four with one dictionary per team.
4. Give each team a photocopy of the prepared Dictionary Relay chart with the target words.
5. The teams complete the chart.
6. The first team to complete the chart completely and correctly wins.

From Allen, K.A. (with Neuhaus, G.F., & Beckwith, M.C.). (2011). Alphabet knowledge: Letter recognition, naming, and sequencing. In J.R. Birsh (Ed.), *Multisensory teaching of basic language skills* (3rd ed., p. 145). Baltimore: Paul H. Brookes Publishing Co.; adapted by permission.

Terms for Phonological Awareness and Alphabet Knowledge

Match each term with the correct definition. Use Chapters 5 and 6 in Birsh (2011) for reference.

1. _____ phonetics
2. _____ phonology
3. _____ allophone
4. _____ phonological awareness
5. _____ phonics
6. _____ phoneme
7. _____ phonemic awareness
8. _____ alphabetic principle
9. _____ quartile
10. _____ grapheme
11. _____ consonant
12. _____ vowel
13. _____ RAN
14. _____ double deficit
15. _____ guided discovery

a. Smallest unit of sound in a syllable
b. Instruction that connects sounds and letters
c. The rules that determine how sounds are used in spoken language
d. Study of the characteristics of speech sounds
e. The understanding that spoken sounds are represented in print by letters
f. Awareness of the overall sound structure of words
g. A variation of a speech sound
h. Awareness of speech sounds or phonemes in spoken words
i. Rapid automatized naming
j. A class of speech sounds with air flow that is constricted or obstructed
k. A method of leading students to new learning through questioning
l. A letter or letter cluster that represents a single speech sound
m. A class of open speech sounds produced by the passage of air through an open vocal tract
n. Deficit in phonological awareness and rapid naming
o. A division of the alphabet that matches the four equal divisions of the dictionary

Planning Lessons for Phonological Awareness, Alphabet Knowledge, and History of Language

A daily lesson plan is needed to organize information for presentation (Birsh & Schedler, 2011). Usually, the first day is a review or a probe of known skills. The subsequent lessons introduce new information or extend and refine known and new skills. Using the charts provided below, plan 5 days of activities for oral language and phonological awareness, alphabet knowledge, and word origin. Use Chapters 4, 5, and 6 in Birsh (2011) for reference.

Oral language and phonological awareness

Day 1	Day 2	Day 3	Day 4	Day 5

(continued on next page)

Alphabet knowledge

Day 1	Day 2	Day 3	Day 4	Day 5

Word origin

Day 1	Day 2	Day 3	Day 4	Day 5

Visit http://library.readingteachersnetwork.org/webinars/small-group-intervention-letter-recognition-and-phonological-awareness to view a webinar on small group intervention of letter recognition and phonological awareness.

Continuous Manuscript Handwriting

The use of continuous manuscript handwriting allows for more fluid movement without the need to lift the pencil during the formation of a letter. Knowledge of correct letter formations facilitates the legibility and speed of handwriting. The use of stroke descriptions aids students in forming letters correctly.

Write the manuscript form of each letter on the line immediately to the right of the printed letter. Match the stroke descriptions with the appropriate letter.

1. b _____	a.	Across, around, stop.
2. m _____	b.	Slant down, up, down, up.
3. l _____	c.	Down, up, around.
4. s _____	d.	Around, stop.
5. z _____	e.	Curve, slant, curve.
6. d _____	f.	Down, hump, hump.
7. e _____	g.	Slant down, slant up.
8. v _____	h.	Across, slant, across.
9. o _____	i.	Down, dot.
10. i _____	j.	Around, close.
11. c _____	k.	Around, up, down.
12. w _____	l.	Down.

Approach Strokes for Cursive Letters

Cursive lowercase letters can be grouped by four approach strokes: *Swing up, stop; Push up and over; Curve under, over, stop;* and *Curve way up, loop left.* Write the lowercase form of each cursive letter of the alphabet according to its approach stroke. See Chapter 7 in Birsh (2011) for further discussion of cursive approach strokes.

Swing up, stop.

Push up and over.

Curve under, over, stop.

Curve way up, loop left.

Approach stroke diagrams courtesy of Luke Waites Center for Dyslexia and Learning Disorders. Texas Scottish Rite Hospital for Children, Child Development Division. (1996). *Teaching cursive writing* [Brochure]. Dallas, TX; Author; adapted by permission.

Cursive Handwriting Stroke Descriptions

Write the cursive form of each letter on the line immediately to the right of the printed letter. On the line to the right of each cursive form, write the letter that corresponds with the matching stroke description. Note that stroke descriptions can vary (e.g., more or fewer words). The idea is to give students verbal support for forming the letters.

1. i _____ _____

2. e _____ _____

3. l _____ _____

4. t _____ _____

5. c _____ _____

6. x _____ _____

7. a _____ _____

8. s _____ _____

9. j _____ _____

10. h _____ _____

11. m _____ _____

12. o _____ _____

a. Swing way up, pull straight down, release, cross.

b. Curve up and over, stop, trace back around and close.

c. Swing up, loop left, pull straight down, release.

d. Swing way up, loop left, pull straight down, release.

e. Swing way up, loop left, pull straight down, push up and over, pull straight down, release.

f. Curve up and over, stop, trace back, down around, release.

g. Swing up, stop, pull way down straight, loop left, curve up and over, dot.

h. Push up and over, slant down, release, slant down left.

i. Swing up, stop, pull straight down, release, dot.

j. Curve up and over, stop, trace back down around and close, pull straight down, release.

k. Swing up, stop, curve down around, close, release.

l. Push up and over, pull straight down, stop, push up and over, pull straight down, stop, push up and over, pull straight down, release.

Handwriting Practice

Handwriting instruction needs to be explicit and systematic (Wolf, 2011). It is brief but regular and focused. As students learn the names and sounds of letters, they connect that information kinesthetically by writing the letters.

Handwriting practice begins with a focus on single letters and then progresses to connecting letters in series and words. Students begin with writing letters using large muscle movements and progressing to smaller models and proper proportion. Students trace, copy from a near-point model, write letters without a model, and copy from a far-point model. When connecting letters, it is helpful for students first to practice connecting letters that share the same approach strokes. Students should always name the letter(s) before writing.

On the following chart, write the introduction and practice handwriting activities listed below hierarchically. The first five activities that are written on the chart can be used for introduction and practice of a letter. Use Chapter 7 in Birsh (2011) for reference.

- Students copy words from the board.
- Students sky write a new letter while looking at a model. The teacher describes the letter strokes.
- Students write letters with attention to proportion.
- Students write a dictated series of letters that share the same approach stroke.
- Students trace a model of the new letter several times with their fingers.
- Students write a dictated series of letters that contain different approach strokes.
- Students trace a model of a new letter with a pencil.
- Students write a new letter from memory.
- Students trace a model of a series of letters that share the same approach stroke.
- Students trace a model of a series of letters that contain different approach strokes.
- Students copy a model of new letter on paper.

Introduction and practice activities
1.
2.
3.
4.
5.

(continued on next page)

Practice activities
6.
7.
8.
9.
10.
11.

Planning Lessons for Handwriting

Use Chapters 7 and 15 in Birsh (2011) for reference and plan 5 days of cursive handwriting activities for the letter *p*. The letters *i*, *s*, and *t* have been introduced and practiced.

Handwriting

Day 1	Day 2	Day 3	Day 4	Day 5

Sound–Symbol Correspondences

The approximately 44 phonemes of English are represented by the 26 letters of the alphabet. Some letters represent graphemes with one frequent sound or a one-to-one correspondence. Some letters represent graphemes with more than one frequent sound. Sort the letters of the alphabet into those letters that can represent graphemes with one frequent sound and those that can represent graphemes with more than one frequent sound. Activity 37 builds on this exercise, but do not turn to that activity until after you have finished this activity.

One frequent sound	More than one frequent sound
1. _____	1. _____
2. _____	2. _____
3. _____	3. _____
4. _____	4. _____
5. _____	5. _____
6. _____	6. _____
7. _____	7. _____
8. _____	8. _____
9. _____	9. _____
10. _____	10. _____
11. _____	11. _____
12. _____	
13. _____	
14. _____	
15. _____	

Practice Words

Awareness of speech sounds and recognition of letters provide the foundation for letter–symbol correspondences. Students begin to read words when they know a few letter–sound correspondences. Initially, practice words should be limited to letters that have been introduced. Generate 68 real practice base words[a] with three or four letters, such as *dog, flip,* or *last,* that can be generated by using only the letters listed below.

a = /ă/   d = /d/   f = /f/   g = /g/   h = /h/   i = /ĭ/   l = /l/   n = /n/   o = /ŏ/   p = /p/   s = /s/   t = /t/

1. _____

2. _____

3. _____

4. _____

5. _____

6. _____

7. _____

8. _____

9. _____

10. _____

11. _____

12. _____

13. _____

14. _____

15. _____

16. _____

17. _____

18. _____

19. _____

20. _____

21. _____

22. _____

23. _____

24. _____

25. _____

26. _____

27. _____

28. _____

29. _____

30. _____

31. _____

32. _____

33. _____

34. _____

35. _____

36. _____

37. _____

38. _____

39. _____

40. _____

41. _____

42. _____

43. _____

44. _____

45. _____

46. _____

47. _____

48. _____

49. _____

50. _____

51. _____

52. _____

53. _____

54. _____

55. _____

56. _____

57. _____

58. _____

59. _____

60. _____

61. _____

62. _____

63. _____

64. _____

65. _____

66. _____

67. _____

68. _____

[a]Older students, however, benefit from the use of nonsense words or pseudowords, as these students may be able to recognize many one-syllable words on sight. The use of nonsense words or pseudowords demonstrates the students' understanding of sound–symbol correspondences.

Writing Dialogues to Make Words

As students learn letter–sound correspondences, they need to practice using them. Students can arrange letter tiles or cards to make words. The teacher begins with a core word, and students change or add one letter at a time to create new words. Write dialogues that move students through several words that use the letters and sounds from Activity 34:

a = /ă/   d = /d/   f = /f/   g = /g/   h = /h/   i = /ĭ/   l = /l/   n = /n/   o = /ŏ/   p = /p/   s = /s/   t = /t/

Follow the example:

Dialogue: Find the letters that spell *at*.
Add the letter that says /p/ and read the word. (*pat*)
Change /p/ to /s/ and read the word. (*sat*)
Change /a/ to /i/ and read the word. (*sit*)
Change /t/ to /p/ and read the word. (*sip*)
Change /s/ to /t/ and read the word. (*tip*)
Change /ĭ/ to /ŏ/ and read the word. (*top*)

Dialogue:
Find the letters that spell *in*.
Add the letter that says /p/. (*pin*)
Change /p/ to /___/. (_____)
Change /___/ to /___/. (_____)
Change /___/ to /___/. (_____)
Change /___/ to /___/. (_____)
Change /___/ to /___/. (_____)

Dialogue:
Find the letters that spell *an*.
Add the letter that says /f/. (*fan*)
Change /f/ to /___/. (_____)
Change /___/ to /___/. (_____)
Change /___/ to /___/. (_____)
Change /___/ to /___/. (_____)
Change /___/ to /___/. (_____)

Dialogue:
Find the letters that spell *it*.
Add the letter that says /s/. (*sit*)
Change /s/ to /___/. (_____)
Change /___/ to /___/. (_____)
Change /__/ to /____/. (_____)
Change /___/ to /___/. (_____)
Change /___/ to /___/. (_____).

Dialogue:
Find the letters that spell *id*.
Add the letter that says /l/. (*lid*)
Change /l/ to /___/. (_____)
Change /___/ to /___/. (_____)
Change /___/ to /___/. (_____)
Change /___/ to /___/. (_____)
Change /___/ to /___/. (_____)

Dialogue:
Find the letters that spell *ad*.
Add the letter that says /h/. (*had*)
Change /h/ to /___/. (_____)
Change /___/ to /___/. (_____)
Change /___/ to /___/. (_____)
Change /___/ to /___/. (_____)

Dialogue:
Find the letters that spell *ig*.
Add the letter that says /f/. (*fig*)
Change /f/ to /___/. (_____)
Change /___/ to /___/. (_____)
Change /___/ to /___/. (_____)
Change /___/ to /___/. (_____)
Change /___/ to /___/. (_____)

(continued on next page)

Dialogue:
Find the letters that spell *og*.
Add the letter that says /d/. (*dog*)
Change /d/ to /___/. (_____)
Change /___/ to /___/. (_____)
Change /___/ to /___/. (_____)
Change /___/ to /___/. (_____)
Change /___/ to /___/. (_____)

Dialogue:
Find the letters that spell *ap*.
Add the letter that says /n/. (*nap*)
Change /p/ to /___/. (_____)
Change /___/ to /___/. (_____)
Change /___/ to /___/. (_____)
Change /___/ to /___/. (_____)
Change /___/ to /___/. (_____)

Dialogue:
Find the letters that spell *op*.
Add the letter that says /s/. (*sop*)
Change /s/ to /___/. (_____)
Change /___/ to /___/. (_____)
Change /___/ to /___/. (_____)
Change /___/ to /___/. (_____)
Change /___/ to /___/. (_____)

Dialogue:
Find the letters that spell *ip*.
Add the letter that says /s/. (*sip*)
Change /s/ to /___/. (_____)
Change /___/ to /___/. (_____)
Change /___/ to /___/. (_____)
Change /___/ to /___/. (_____)
Change /___/ to /___/. (_____)

Planning Lessons for Beginning Reading

A daily lesson plan organizes information for presentation (Birsh & Schedler, 2011). Often, the first day's activity in a weekly lesson is a review or a probe of known skills. The subsequent days' lessons introduce new information or extend and refine known and new skills. Plan 3 days of new concept introduction and review activities. A review activity and a concept introduction have been planned for you. Plan 4 days of reading practice activities that reinforce known skills. The first reading practice has been planned for you.

For the purposes of planning, assume that the students have learned the short vowels *a* and *i* and the consonants *d, f, g, h, l, n, p, s,* and *t*. The next three letter introductions are short vowel *o* and consonants *m* and *b*. Plan the reviews of previously introduced concepts and the introductions of the new letters and sounds. Decide on which day students will review, on which day you will introduce *m*, and on which day you will introduce *b*. Based on what students know, what words could students read each day? Make a list of 15 words for each day. Use only those letters that have been introduced. Activity 34 will be helpful in creating the lists of words. Decide if students will read words on the board or on paper or will use letter tiles and cards to make and read words as demonstrated in Activity 35 . Introducing new concepts and reading practice activities are explained in Carreker (2011a). Refer to the lesson plan models in Figures 15.1 through 15.4 in Chapter 15 (Birsh, 2011).

New Concept Introduction or Review

Day 1	Day 2	Day 3	Day 4	Day 5
Review – students repeat sequences of sounds and blend them into words. For example, /n/ /ă/ /p/ /s/ /n/ /ă/ /p/ /s/ /p/ /ĭ/ /t/ /s/ /p/ /ĭ/ /n/	Introduce short vowel /ŏ/. Discovery words: *off toss* *on soft* *frost* Key word: *octopus*			

(continued on next page)

Reading Practice

Day 1	Day 2	Day 3	Day 4	Day 5
Students will read words on a reading practice page. *hit pats* *hip past* *hiss last* *hips fast* *sip flap* *slip slat* *snip slap* *spin pins*				

As noted in Activity 33, some letters have more than one frequent sound. Pronouncing a letter with more than one sound may be determined by the position of the letter in a word and/or the occurrence of the letter with other letters (Carreker, 2011a; Cox, 1992). You will discover that patterns for five letters have more than one frequent pronunciation. Read the words below that contain the same letter. There are multiple pronunciations for the letter. How do you know which pronunciation to use? Decide the pattern that dictates the pronunciation of each letter and write the pattern. The first pattern is done for you.

PATTERN 1

When is *c* pronounced /k/ and when is *c* pronounced /s/?

cat	*cent*
cycle	*clasp*
cup	*cot*
city	*crib*

c is pronounced /k/ <u>before a, o, u, or any consonant</u>

c is pronounced /s/ _____

PATTERN 2

When is *g* pronounced /g/ and when is *g* pronounced /j/?

gate	*glad*
gypsy	*gist*
gum	*gym*
gem	*got*

g is pronounced /g/ _____

g is pronounced /j/ _____

PATTERN 3

When is *n* pronounced /n/ and when is *n* pronounced /ng/?

nap	*snip*
sink	*sanctuary*
finger	*vanquish*
angle	*spin*

n is pronounced /n/ _____

n is pronounced /ng/ _____

(continued on next page)

PATTERN 4

When is *x* pronounced /ks/ and when is *x* pronounced /z/?

xylophone	*exit*
expel	*xylem*
xenophobia	*box*
relax	

x is pronounced /ks/ _____

x is pronounced /z/ _____

PATTERN 5

When is *y* pronounced /y/, when is *y* pronounced /ī /, and when is *y* pronounced /ē/?

fly	*reply*	*yellow*
yank	*yield*	*yogurt*
empty	*shy*	*penny*
supply	*Yule*	*happy*

y is pronounced /y/ _____

y is pronounced /ī / _____

y is pronounced /ē/ _____

Hard and Soft *c* and *g*

The letter *c* can represent the hard sound /k/ or the soft sound /s/. The letter *g* can represent the hard sound /g/ or the soft sound /j/. Look at the underlined letter in each word below. Check the sounds that the letter represents as hard or soft. Write the pattern that determines that the letter is hard or soft.

	Hard	Soft	Pattern
city		✓	*c before i is pronounced /s/*
gem			
clown			
cent			
fancy			
gym			
gist			
space			
energy			
inclusion			
exigent			
facility			
gentleman			
bicycle			
bicycle			
difficult			
registration			

Label each consonant pair as a *consonant blend*, which retains the individual sounds of each letter, or a *consonant digraph*, which represents one sound:

1. *bl* _____

2. *sh* _____

3. *mp* _____

4. *th* _____

5. *nk* _____

6. *nt* _____

7. *ck* _____

8. *wh* _____

9. *ch* _____

10. *dr* _____

Label each vowel pair as a *digraph*, which consists of two adjacent vowels that represent one sound, or a *diphthong*, which contains two adjacent vowels with a slide or a shift in the middle of the pronunciation.

11. *ea* _____

12. *oi* _____

13. *ou* _____

14. *oe* _____

15. *ai* _____

16. *oy* _____

17. *oo* _____

18. *oa* _____

19. *au* _____

20. *aw* _____

How Many Letters and
How Many Graphemes?

Letters are symbols. Graphemes are single letters or letter groups that represent specific phonemes or speech sounds. Write the number of letters and the number of graphemes for each word.

		Letters	Graphemes			Letters	Graphemes
1.	bridge	_____	_____	11.	breath	_____	_____
2.	wheel	_____	_____	12.	slant	_____	_____
3.	church	_____	_____	13.	stack	_____	_____
4.	school	_____	_____	14.	shack	_____	_____
5.	show	_____	_____	15.	sketch	_____	_____
6.	band	_____	_____	16.	hand	_____	_____
7.	feet	_____	_____	17.	finish	_____	_____
8.	knife	_____	_____	18.	straw	_____	_____
9.	phone	_____	_____	19.	head	_____	_____
10.	song	_____	_____	20.	shroud	_____	_____

How Many Letters and How Many Graphemes?

TEXTBOOK REFERENCE
Chapters 5, 6, 8, and 16

Letters are symbols. Graphemes are single letters or letter groups that represent specific phonemes or speech sounds. Write the number of letters and the number of graphemes for each word.

		Letters	Graphemes				Letters	Graphemes
1.	deck	_____	_____		11.	teacher	_____	_____
2.	lamp	_____	_____		12.	phone	_____	_____
3.	bench	_____	_____		13.	sports	_____	_____
4.	smoke	_____	_____		14.	plate	_____	_____
5.	glow	_____	_____		15.	stretch	_____	_____
6.	shrine	_____	_____		16.	strand	_____	_____
7.	cheese	_____	_____		17.	clover	_____	_____
8.	pencil	_____	_____		18.	start	_____	_____
9.	state	_____	_____		19.	seed	_____	_____
10.	strong	_____	_____		20.	threat	_____	_____

Vowel Pairs

The adage "When two vowels go walking, the first one does the talking" works about 45% of the time (Adams, 1990). Sort the vowel pairs listed below as those pairs that follow the adage and those pairs that do not.

ai (*paint*)	ei (*vein*)	oo (*book*)
au (*saucer*)	eu (*Europe*)	oo (*moon*)
aw (*saw*)	ew (*pew*)	ou (*out*)
ay (*play*)	ey (*monkey*)	ow (*show*)
ea (*teach*)	ie (*tie*)	ow (*cow*)
ea (*head*)	ie (*priest*)	oy (*boy*)
ea (*steak*)	oa (*boat*)	ue (*statue*)
ee (*feet*)	oe (*toe*)	ui (*fruit*)
ei (*ceiling*)	oi (*oil*)	

The first vowel does the talking	The first vowel does not do the talking
ai (paint)	

Vowel-*r* Patterns

When an *r* comes after a vowel, the vowel makes an unexpected sound. Each vowel situation must be taught. Sort the following vowel-*r* patterns by sound.

ar (*star*), *ar* (*dollar*), *ar* (*warm*), *ar* (*quart*), *er* (*fern*), *er* (*letter*), *ir* (*first*), *ir* (*tapir*), *or* (*fork*), *or* (*doctor*), *or* (*work*), *ur* (*fur*), *ur* (*murmur*)

/er/	/ar/	/or/
ar (*dollar*)		

Generalizations:

The patterns *er, ir,* and *ur* are always pronounced _____.

In an accented syllable *ar* is pronounced _____ and *or* is pronounced _____.

In an unaccented syllable, *ar* and *or* are pronounced _____.

After /w/, *or* is pronounced _____.

After /w/, *ar* is pronounced _____.

Syllable Type Definitions

Most words in English can be categorized as one of six syllable types or as a composite of the different syllable types (Carreker, 2011b): closed, open, vowel-consonant-*e*, vowel-*r* (or *r*-controlled), vowel pair (or vowel team), and consonant-*le*, which is a type of final stable syllable (Stanback, 1992; Steere, Peck, Kahn, 1984). Match each syllable type with its correct characteristics.

1. _____ closed syllable
2. _____ open syllable
3. _____ vowel-consonant-*e* syllable
4. _____ vowel pair syllable
5. _____ vowel-*r* syllable
6. _____ consonant-*le* syllable (a kind of final stable syllable)

a. A syllable that has an *r* after the vowel
b. A nonphonetic, recurring syllable that is fairly stable in its pronunciation and spelling
c. A syllable with two adjacent vowels in initial, medial, or final position
d. A syllable that ends in one vowel and at least one consonant
e. A syllable that ends in one vowel
f. A syllable that ends in one vowel, one consonant, and final *e*

Sorting Syllable Types
Closed, Open, Vowel-*r*

TEXTBOOK REFERENCE
Chapters 8 and 16

Write the words in the appropriate columns, according to the syllable type the word represents. Examples of sorted syllables have been done for you. Refer to Chapter 8 (Birsh, 2011).

Sort open and closed syllables

hiss   sod   so   hen   he   hem   met   me   west   we

Open	Closed
hi	hit

Sort closed and vowel-r syllables

firm   car   fond   hand   spur   spun   cat   fork   hard   fist

Closed	Vowel-*r*

ACTIVITY 46

Sorting Syllable Types
Closed, Open, Vowel Pairs

Write the words in the appropriate columns according to the syllable type the word represents. Use Chapter 8 (Birsh, 2011) as a reference.

Sort closed and vowel pair syllables

miss   seed   toast   help   book   bond   stomp   heap   send   maid

Closed	Vowel pair

Sort open and vowel pair syllables

free   so   fly   deep   moo   be   cry   bee   play   me

Open	Vowel pair

Sorting Syllable Types

Write the following words in the appropriate column. If a word has two syllables, write the word in the two columns that represent the syllable types in the word.

not	here	hive	low	picture	weep
note	her	hi	she	portion	work
nor	hen	hit	sheep	peek	warm
no	mettle	lost	shamble	supreme	my
noon	meet	lone	short	so	mine
noble	me	lore	shine	soak	marble
he	mean	loan	pie	we	
heat	men	locate	pick	went	

Closed	Open	Vowel-consonant-*e*	Vowel-*r*	Vowel pair	Final stable or consonant-*le*

5a   Sorting Syllable Types as a Group Activity

1. Photocopy the Six Syllable Types Chart on page 138 onto card stock, making one chart.
2. Photocopy the card template on page 139 and cut the chart apart into cards.
3. Distribute cards to students.
4. Students take turns identifying the syllable types represented on their cards.
5. Students place each card in the appropriate syllable type column on the chart.
6. As students place each card on the chart, they identify the vowel sound in the target syllable, read the word, and use it in an oral sentence.

The second card template in Appendix F on page 140 can be used separately on another day or can be used with the first card template.

5b   Sorting Syllable Types as an Individual Activity

1. Photocopy the Six Syllable Types Chart on page 138 onto card stock, making one chart for each student.
2. Photocopy the card template on page 139 and cut the chart apart into cards, making one set for each student. Store each card set in a zip-top plastic bag.
3. Distribute cards and card sets in the bags to students.
4. Students work independently, placing each card in the appropriate syllable type column on the chart.
5. When students have finished sorting their cards, check their work by asking students one at a time to identify the vowel sound in the target syllable, read the word, and use it in an oral sentence. Continue in this manner until all the cards have been checked.

The second card template in Appendix F on page 140 can be used separately on another day or can be used with the first card template.

Which Syllable Type?

Identify the syllable type of each word or underlined syllable.

1. lump _____
2. smoke _____
3. she _____
4. speech _____
5. clutch _____
6. strict _____
7. thirst _____
8. porch _____
9. stray _____
10. bott<u>le</u> _____

11. mon<u>ster</u> _____
12. <u>moi</u>sture _____
13. sim<u>ple</u> _____
14. hun<u>dred</u> _____
15. so<u>lo</u> _____
16. <u>per</u>fect _____
17. ex<u>treme</u> _____
18. pub<u>lish</u> _____
19. cir<u>cle</u> _____
20. <u>fre</u>quent _____

TRY THIS

6 Syllable Types Concentration Game

1. Create a concentration game board using the template on page 137.
2. Prepare the game board as an overhead transparency or on an interactive whiteboard.
3. Choose six words or syllables.
4. Write these words or syllables randomly in the empty spaces on the game board.
5. Write the six syllable types that represent each word or syllable randomly in the remaining spaces.
6. Cover each of the squares with small sticky notes.
7. Place the transparency on the overhead projector if using one.
8. Divide students into teams and determine a rotation.
9. Teams take turns calling out pairs of coordinates (e.g., A3 and B3) to search for a word and a syllable type that match.
10. Uncover the spaces that correspond to the coordinates.
11. If the word and syllable type match, the team gets a point.
12. If the word and syllable type do not match, cover the two spaces again with sticky notes.
13. Each team gets only one turn per round, regardless of whether the team has scored a point.
14. The game continues until all of the spaces have been uncovered.

Generating Syllable Types

Generate 10 examples of each of the syllable types.

Closed_____

_____

_____

Open_____

_____

_____

Vowel-consonant-*e*_____

_____

_____

Vowel pair_____

_____

_____

Vowel-*r*_____

_____

_____

Final stable (e.g., consonant-*le*)_____

_____

TRY THIS

7 Syllable Puzzles 1

1. Write the syllables of several two-syllable words on separate index cards. (See pages 141–142 for sample words.)
2. Lay out two cards that form a two-syllable word in random order.
3. Students take turns identifying the syllable type on each card, identifying the vowel sound in each syllable, and reading the syllables.
4. Students arrange the cards into a word. They read the word and use it in a sentence.

You can also do this activity with three-syllable words. (See page 142 for sample words.)

Syllable Division Patterns

There are four major patterns in English that indicate where a word will be divided into syllables: VCCV, VCV, VCCCV, and VV. The VCCV pattern has two consonants between two vowels. The VCV pattern has one consonant between two vowels. The VCCCV pattern has three consonants between two vowels. The VV pattern has two adjacent vowels that do not represent a vowel digraph or a diphthong.

For each word, identify the syllable division pattern: VCCV, VCV, VCCCV, or VV.

1. mascot _VCCV_____

2. rotate _____

3. monster _____

4. bias _____

5. tactic _____

6. cabin _____

7. lion _____

8. supreme _____

9. portray _____

10. second _____

11. pumpkin _____

12. truant _____

13. surround _____

14. instant _____

15. item _____

16. convoy _____

17. instinct _____

18. report _____

19. contrast _____

20. connect _____

Where to Divide Words
VCCV or VCV?

There are patterns in English that indicate where a word will be divided into syllables. The two most common patterns are VCCV and VCV. The VCCV pattern has two consonants between two vowels. A word with this pattern is usually divided between the two consonants but can also be divided after the first vowel. The VCV pattern has one consonant between two vowels. A word with this pattern is usually divided before the consonant but can also be divided after the consonant.

Write each word on the line. Divide the word into syllables.

1. chipmunk _chip munk_____
2. lotus _____
3. distance _____
4. pigment _____
5. entice _____
6. banner _____
7. duty _____
8. detain _____
9. escape _____
10. baby _____

11. party _____
12. provide _____
13. local _____
14. stubborn _____
15. below _____
16. market _____
17. locate _____
18. copper _____
19. relate _____
20. ribbon _____

Visit http://library.readingteachersnetwork.org/lessonets/syllable-division-review-vccv-words and http://library.readingteachersnetwork.org/lessonets/syllable-division-review-vcv-words for lessons on the VCCV and VCV syllable division patterns, respectively.

Where to Divide Words
VCCCV or VV?

TEXTBOOK REFERENCE
Chapters 8 and 16

The four patterns in English for dividing words into syllables are: VCCV, VCV, VCCCV, and VV. The VCCCV pattern has three consonants between two vowels. A word with this pattern is usually divided after the first consonant but can also be divided after the second consonant. The VV pattern has two adjacent vowels that do not represent a vowel digraph or diphthong or pronouncing the adjacent vowels as a digraph or diphthong does not produce a recognizable word (e.g., *stoic* versus *stō /ĭ c*). A word with this pattern is divided between the two vowels.

Write each word on the line. Divide the word into syllables.

1. chaos   *cha os* _____
2. lion _____
3. district _____
4. poem _____
5. extreme _____
6. construct _____
7. duet _____
8. destroy _____
9. pumpkin _____
10. muskrat _____

11. partner _____
12. ruin _____
13. dual _____
14. distract _____
15. bias _____
16. contract _____
17. dais _____
18. truant _____
19. misspell _____
20. spectrum _____

Visit http://library.readingteachersnetwork.org/lessonets/syllable-division-review-vcccv-words and http://library.readingteachersnetwork.org/lessonets/syllable-division-review-vv-words for lessons on the VCCCV and VV syllable division patterns, respectively.

Accent

In most English words, the accent falls on the first syllable. In some words, the accent falls on the second syllable. Accent the proper syllable in the words below.

1. spi der _____
2. bo a _____
3. pre dict _____
4. con stant _____
5. con trol _____
6. na vy _____
7. qui et _____
8. pas tel _____
9. en ter _____
10. can teen _____

11. sev en _____
12. be cause _____
13. cham ber _____
14. con voy _____
15. tri al _____
16. spec trum _____
17. pump kin _____
18. tri umph _____
19. de cide _____
20. chal lenge _____

ACTIVITY 54

Syllable Division Patterns and Choices

There are four major patterns in English that indicate where a word will be divided into syllables: VCCV, VCV, VCCCV, and VV. For each of these four patterns, there are different choices for division and accent placement.

1. The first choice of each pattern involves the most frequent division with the accent on the first syllable.
2. The second choice of each pattern involves the most frequent division with the accent on the second syllable.
3. The third choice of each pattern usually involves a different division with the accent on the first syllable.

Identify the pattern (VCCV, VCV, VCCCV, or VV) and the choice (first, second, or third).

1.	mascot	*VCCV, first*	11.	pumpkin
2.	rotate		12.	truant
3.	monster		13.	surround
4.	bias		14.	instant
5.	tactic		15.	item
6.	cabin		16.	convoy
7.	lion		17.	instinct
8.	supreme		18.	report
9.	portray		19.	contrast
10.	second		20.	connect

TRY THIS

8 Syllable Puzzles 2

1. Write the syllables of several two-syllable words on separate large cards. See pages 141–142 for sample words.
2. Distribute cards among students.
3. Students move around the room and match their syllables to form words.
4. When students have matched syllables to form words, each pair identifies the syllables in the word and reads it.
5. As each pair reads its word, the student holding the accented syllable holds his or her card higher.

You can also do this activity with three-syllable words. (See page 142 for sample words.)

Short Vowels in Vowel-*r* Syllables

A vowel in a vowel-*r* pattern usually makes an unexpected sound, as in *fur, for, car, her,* and *dirt.* These words look like closed syllables, and you would expect to pronounce the vowel in each word as a short vowel. However, when each of these words is pronounced, the vowel is not pronounced as a short vowel. The *r* after the vowel makes the vowel make an unexpected sound. Therefore, these words are referred to as vowel-*r* syllables and not as closed syllables. An *r* after the vowel alerts the reader that the vowel in the combination with *r* will be pronounced as /er/, /ar/, or /or/. When will the vowel in a vowel-*r* pattern be pronounced as a short vowel?

1. In words of two or more syllables, if there is a vowel-*rr* pattern, the word will divide between the two *r*'s and the vowel in the vowel-*r* pattern will be pronounced as a short vowel as in *barrel* or *errand.*
2. In a word of two or more syllables, if there is a vowel-*r*-vowel pattern and the word divides after the *r*, the vowel in the vowel-*r* pattern will be pronounced as a short vowel as in *perish* or *parable.* (To determine that a word such as *perish* divides after the *r*, the reader has already determined that dividing before the *r* does not produce a recognizable word: /pē' rish/ or /pē rish'/.)

All the following words have vowel-*r* patterns. Write the pronunciation of the vowel in each vowel-*r* pattern. The first two examples have been done for you.

1. me<u>rr</u>y   */ĕ/* _____
2. co<u>rne</u>r   */or /er/* _____
3. fi<u>rs</u>t _____
4. ca<u>rr</u>y _____
5. ve<u>r</u>y _____
6. su<u>rv</u>ey _____
7. che<u>rr</u>y _____
8. e<u>rr</u>and _____
9. ga<u>rl</u>ic _____
10. de<u>rr</u>ick _____
11. fe<u>rr</u>et _____
12. she<u>rb</u>et _____
13. me<u>r</u>it _____
14. ba<u>rr</u>ack _____
15. ha<u>rn</u>ess _____
16. e<u>rr</u>or _____
17. o<u>rb</u>it _____
18. ca<u>rr</u>ot _____
19. u<u>rg</u>ent _____
20. na<u>rr</u>ow _____

Match the examples with the appropriate terms:

1. _____ -ed
2. _____ -ful
3. _____ igh
4. _____ ou, ow, oi, oy
5. _____ /t/ and /d/
6. _____ st, mp, br, dr
7. _____ pin<u>s</u>
8. _____ eigh
9. _____ ad-
10. _____ port
11. _____ struct
12. _____ m<u>et</u>
13. _____ tip<u>s</u>
14. _____ -ist
15. _____ uni-
16. _____ <u>m</u>et

a. bound morpheme
b. consonant suffix
c. vowel prefix
d. blends
e. trigraph
f. quadrigraph
g. unvoiced suffix -s
h. free morpheme
i. diphthongs
j. inflectional ending
k. cognates
l. onset
m. voiced suffix -s
n. consonant prefix
o. vowel suffix
p. rime

Vowel and Consonant Suffixes

A suffix is a letter or group of letters added to the end of a base word. A suffix that begins with a vowel is referred to as a *vowel suffix*. It is important to be able to identify suffixes because, when a vowel suffix is added to the end of a base word, the spelling of the base word may change. A suffix that begins with a consonant is referred to as a *consonant suffix*. Sort the following suffixes as vowel or consonant suffixes:

-en, -ment, -ful, -ity, -ous, -ness, -less, -able, -ish, -ly, -ist, -ward.

Vowel suffixes	**Consonant suffixes**
_____	_____
_____	_____
_____	_____
_____	_____
_____	_____
_____	_____

Inflectional Ending -*s*

The letter -*s* after a base word that is a verb represents an inflectional ending. For purposes of decoding, this ending acts as a suffix that is added to a base word and indicates the third person singular. The inflectional ending -*s* has two different pronunciations, /s/ or /z/. After an unvoiced speech sound, it is pronounced /s/. After a voiced speech sound, it is pronounced /z/. Place a check mark in the column corresponding to the correct pronunciation of the ending -*s* —/s/ or /z/—for each of these derivatives.

		/s/	**/z/**
1.	seems	_____	_____
2.	jumps	_____	_____
3.	lands	_____	_____
4.	starts	_____	_____
5.	lists	_____	_____
6.	picks	_____	_____
7.	likes	_____	_____
8.	settles	_____	_____
9.	copes	_____	_____
10.	spells	_____	_____
11.	camps	_____	_____
12.	distributes	_____	_____
13.	recycles	_____	_____
14.	screams	_____	_____
15.	grasps	_____	_____

Inflectional Ending -ed

The letters -ed after a base word represent an inflectional ending. For the purposes of decoding, this ending acts as a suffix that is added to a base word and indicates the past tense. The inflectional ending -ed has three different pronunciations, /ĕd/, /t/, or /d/. After the letters t or d, the ending is pronounced /ĕd/. After an unvoiced sound, the ending is pronounced /t/. After a voiced sound, the ending is pronounced /d/. Place a check mark in the column corresponding to the correct pronunciation of ending -ed for each of these derivatives.

		/ĕd/	/t/	/d/
1.	seemed	_____	_____	_____
2.	jumped	_____	_____	_____
3.	landed	_____	_____	_____
4.	started	_____	_____	_____
5.	tossed	_____	_____	_____
6.	picked	_____	_____	_____
7.	listed	_____	_____	_____
8.	settled	_____	_____	_____
9.	copied	_____	_____	_____
10.	spelled	_____	_____	_____
11.	camped	_____	_____	_____
12.	distributed	_____	_____	_____
13.	recycled	_____	_____	_____
14.	enclosed	_____	_____	_____
15.	realized	_____	_____	_____

Inflectional and Derivational Suffixes

Inflectional suffixes are added to a base word or root and create a new word that is the same part of speech as the base word. Derivational suffixes are added to a base word or root and create a new word that is different from the base word in terms of part of speech or function (Moats, 1995, 2000). Derivational suffixes change the meaning, form, or usage of the base word.

Write the part of speech of each base word. Write the part of speech of each derivative. Write the ending or suffix that was added to the base word. Mark whether the suffix is an inflectional or derivational suffix.

Base word	Part of speech	Derivative	Part of speech	Ending or suffix	Inflectional	Derivational
desk	noun	desks	noun	-s	✓	
help		helpless				
big		bigger				
mow		mowing				
play		playful				
sky		skies				
bleed		bleeding				
copy		copying				
dark		darkness				
keep		keeper				
merry		merriment				

Irregular Words for Reading

Irregular words contain orthographic patterns whose pronunciations do not match the most frequent pronunciations for those patterns. For each word listed, circle the orthographic representation whose pronunciation does not match the most frequent pronunciation.

1. sh(oe)
2. country
3. busy
4. ghost
5. lamb
6. said
7. does
8. doubt
9. four

10. ocean
11. enough
12. aisle
13. friend
14. plaid
15. from
16. would
17. two
18. colonel

Regular or Irregular for Reading?

Words that follow the reliable sound–spelling patterns of the language are regular. Words that do not follow the reliable sound–spelling patterns are irregular. Read each word and mark it with *R* for regular or *I* for irregular.

1.	done	_____	11.	lose	_____
2.	down	_____	12.	lone	_____
3.	one	_____	13.	back	_____
4.	tone	_____	14.	buy	_____
5.	again	_____	15.	pretty	_____
6.	paint	_____	16.	plenty	_____
7.	seed	_____	17.	become	_____
8.	seat	_____	18.	began	_____
9.	came	_____	19.	any	_____
10.	come	_____	20.	orange	_____

9 Irregular Word Procedure

1. Write an irregular word on the board.
2. Students identify the syllable type and code the word according to the regular patterns of reading. Students read the word and discover it does not follow the reliable patterns of the language.
3. Erase the coded word and rewrite the word on the board. Beside the word, write the pronunciation in parentheses.
4. Students compare the word and the pronunciation and decide which part is irregular.
5. Circle the irregular part.
6. Write the word on the front of a 4" × 6" index card. On the back of the card, write the pronunciation. Cut off the upper left-hand corner of the front of the card. The irregular shape of the card cues students that the word printed on it is an irregular word.
7. Hold up the card so that students see the front of the card. Students read the word aloud.
8. Turn the card around. Students read the pronunciation aloud.
9. Slowly turn the card from front to back four or five times as students read the word and then read the pronunciation aloud.
10. Add the card to a deck of irregular words that is reviewed daily.

From Carreker, S. (2011a). Teaching reading: Accurate decoding. In J.R. Birsh (Ed.), *Multisensory teaching of basic language skills* (3rd ed., p. 207). Baltimore: Paul H. Brookes Publishing Co.; adapted by permission.

Regular or Irregular for Reading?

Read each word and mark it with *R* for regular sound–spelling pattern or *I* for irregular sound–spelling pattern.

1.	couch	_____	13. people	_____
2.	some	_____	14. queen	_____
3.	whose	_____	15. between	_____
4.	could	_____	16. together	_____
5.	sole	_____	17. trouble	_____
6.	soul	_____	18. tremble	_____
7.	eye	_____	19. woman	_____
8.	many	_____	20. were	_____
9.	trust	_____	21. should	_____
10.	truth	_____	22. where	_____
11.	debt	_____	23. why	_____
12.	dead	_____	24. match	_____

ACTIVITY 64

The Art and Science of Fluency Instruction

TEXTBOOK REFERENCE
Chapters 8 and 10

Students' difficulties with fluency will be manifested differently. To become fluent, a reader's instruction must meet his or her needs. Figure 3 is a case study from Chapter 10 (Birsh, 2011). Determine the reader's strengths and weaknesses and appropriate strategies and activities for improving fluency.

Geoffrey

Geoffrey, a wiry 11-year-old boy, scored mid-2nd grade on reading measures when he entered our after-school tutoring lab. He was a wild guesser, self-deprecating, and full of "No, no, wait...." His early schooling had emphasized re-reading leveled trade books of motivating children's literature, with the stunning result that Geoffrey could read several books from memory, without recognizing their constituent words in any other context.

Geoff and his tutor began by building his word recognition foundation: letter sounds (especially vowels), blending, segmenting, word analogies, and syllable patterns. Geoffrey loved the daily word-card practice and charting his increasing speed. Then his tutor introduced phrase and sentence practice. Results: an astounding slowdown. Words Geoff had read with alacrity during word-card drills, when they were strung together in meaningful phrases and sentences, he now read them as if his mental joints had rusted over. It was fascinating that this slowdown was the opposite of what happens with many other kids, whose reading gets more fluent in context with the support of phrase structure and the flow of sense. Instead, for Geoff, the words racing one-after-another-after-another in the continuous flow of text resulted in a glacial slowdown. When he tried speeding up, he became, once again, wildly inaccurate.

Figure 3. Geoffrey and the glacial slowdown in continuous text.

What are Geoffrey's strengths?

(continued on next page)

What are Geoffrey's needs?

_____

_____

_____

_____

_____

_____

_____

_____

_____

_____

_____

_____

_____

_____

What instructional strategies and activities would best improve Geoffrey's fluency?

_____

_____

_____

_____

_____

_____

_____

_____

_____

_____

_____

_____

Measuring Prosody

Chapter 8 of Birsh (2011) outlines procedures for measuring reading rate, or how many words are read correctly in 1 minute. Prosody, the flow and expression of students' reading, also can be measured. To make an objective judgment, you can create a prosody rubric with different features to assess. Features of prosody include:

- Using correct intonation for text marked by ending punctuation marks
- Pausing at commas
- Grouping words into meaningful units
- Adjusting stress and pitch to reflect comprehension

Points are given for use of correct intonation and pausing that is marked by punctuation. Points are given for phrasing words into meaningful units and for adjusting stress and pitch to reflect comprehension, such as in a dialogue. Decide what features are present in the first 50 words of a passage and assign a point value for different features. For example, if there are three commas in the first 50 words, the feature recorded as pausing at commas could have a point value of 3, with 1 point for each comma. Ideally, all four features of prosody are measured in a passage, although the point values for the features may vary.

Feature	Point value
Using correct intonation for text marked by ending punctuation marks	
Pausing at commas	
Grouping words into meaningful units	
Adjusting stress and pitch to reflect comprehension	

Look at the passage in Figure 4 on the next page. Mark the 50th word with an asterisk. Based on the features in those 50 words, make a rubric with a 10-point total.

(continued on next page)

The Crow and the Pitcher

Once a thirsty crow came upon a pitcher and heaved a sigh of relief, "At last I shall quench my unquenchable thirst."

When the crow put his beak into the pitcher, he found he could not reach the water, for there was just a little bit of water left. No matter how hard he tried, he could not reach down far enough to get the water.

The crow was about to give up when a thought came to him. He began to pick up pebbles one at a time and drop them into the pitcher.

Each pebble made the water rise closer to the brim. Finally the water mounted to the brim. The crow perched himself on the handle of the pitcher and drank until he was no longer thirsty.

Figure 4. A passage for measuring prosody. (From Carreker, S. [2004]. *Developing metacognitive skill: Vocabulary and comprehension*. Bellaire, TX: Neuhaus Education Center; reprinted by permission. Copyright © 2004 by Neuhaus Education Center. All rights reserved.)

As students read, give points for the features that are present in students' oral reading. A prosody scale is developed that might look like this:

Prosody scale	
9–10 points	Fluent
7–8 points	Nearly fluent
5–6 points	Progressing
3–4 points	Beginning fluency
0–2 points	Not fluent

With a prosody scale, you will have a measure of speed and accuracy (i.e., how many words a student reads correctly per minute) and a measure of prosody (i.e., the quality of the flow with which a student reads).

Terms for Decoding and Fluency

Match each term with the correct definition.

1. _____ synthetic
2. _____ analytic
3. _____ morpheme
4. _____ syllable
5. _____ explicit instruction
6. _____ blend
7. _____ coarticulation
8. _____ fluency
9. _____ exaggerated pronunciation
10. _____ prosody
11. _____ macron
12. _____ breve
13. _____ irregular word
14. _____ digraph
15. _____ diphthong
16. _____ corrective feedback

a. Direct, purposeful instruction
b. The rhythmic flow of oral reading
c. A word with an unexpected pronunciation or spelling
d. A unit of speech
e. Two adjacent letters in the same syllable that represent one sound
f. A diacritical marking for a long vowel
g. Pertaining to parts that build to a whole
h. A meaning unit of language
i. Two or more letters whose sounds flow smoothly together
j. A diacritical marking for a short vowel
k. Two adjacent vowels in the same syllable whose sounds blend together with a slide or shift during production
l. Reading with rapidity and automaticity
m. The overpronunciation of a word to aid memory
n. The overlapping of adjacent sounds when spoken
o. Pertaining to a whole that is broken into constituent parts
p. Immediate teacher response to student performance that is sensitive to the student's level of skill

TRY THIS

10 Rapid Word-Recognition Chart

1. Make a photocopy of the Rapid Word-Recognition Chart on page 149.
2. Fill the chart with six words that repeat in a different order in each row.
3. Prepare the chart as an overhead transparency or on an interactive whiteboard.
4. Touch and read the words in the first row.
5. Touch the words in the first row as students read them.
6. Start again at the top. Touch the words as quickly possible, working across each row and down the chart, row by row.
7. Time the students for 1 minute.
8. The initial goal is for students to read the chart two times in 1 minute. Eventually, the goal for students in grades 3 and higher is to read the chart four times in 1 minute.

Source: Carreker (2011a).

ACTIVITY 67

Spelling Patterns

Some sounds in English have one spelling or one overwhelmingly recurring spelling. When a sound has more than one frequent spelling pattern (e.g., /oi/ can be spelled *oi* or *oy*), the best choice of the pattern is based on the frequency of a particular spelling pattern and the situation of the sound in the word. The situation of the sound may be based on the position of the sound in the word, the placement of accent, the length of the words, the influences of surrounding sounds, or a combination of these factors (Carreker, 1992; 2011a; Hanna, Hanna, & Hodges, 1964).

Match the spelling patterns and the situation.

1. _____	Final /k/ is spelled *ck*	a.	after *w*
2. _____	/k/ is spelled *k*	b.	in final position of a one-syllable word
3. _____	/ā/ is spelled *ay*	c.	in final position
4. _____	/ŏ/ is spelled *a*	d.	after a short vowel in a multisyllabic word
5. _____	/ē/ is spelled *ee*	e.	after a short vowel in a one-syllable word
6. _____	Final /k/ is spelled *c*	f.	before *e, i,* or *y*

Match the spelling patterns and the situation.

7. _____	/ē/ is spelled *y*	g.	at the end of a word or an unaccented syllable
8. _____	/ŭ/ is spelled *a*	h.	in final position
9. _____	/ou/ is spelled *ou*	i.	in initial or medial position
10. _____	/er/ is spelled *or*	j.	at the end of a two-syllable word
11. _____	/ū/ is spelled *ue*	k.	at the end of a syllable
12. _____	/ī/ is spelled *i*	l.	after *w*

Match the spelling patterns and the situation.

13. _____	/oi/ is spelled *oi*	m.	in initial or medial position
14. _____	/j/ is spelled *g*	n.	at the end of a syllable
15. _____	/ch/ is spelled *tch*	o.	in initial or medial position of a one-syllable word or medial position of a final syllable in a multisyllabic word
16. _____	/ō/ is spelled *ow*	p.	after a short vowel in a one-syllable word
17. _____	/ō/ is spelled *o*-consonant-*e*	q.	before *e, i,* or *y*
18. _____	/ū/ is spelled *u*	r.	in final position

Identifying Spelling Patterns

Write the sound that is represented with the underlined letter or letters and the pattern that determines the use of the letter or letters to represent that sound. Use Chapter 9 in Birsh (2011) for reference.

		Sound	Spelling pattern
1.	emp**loy**	/oi/	final /oi/ is spelled oy
2.	gr**ou**nd	_____	_____
3.	**g**iant	_____	_____
4.	gr**ee**n	_____	_____
5.	mat**ch**	_____	_____
6.	tun**a**	_____	_____
7.	p**o**lite	_____	_____
8.	**c**andy	_____	_____
9.	lila**c**	_____	_____
10.	ug**l**y	_____	_____
11.	por**ch**	_____	_____
12.	sh**y**	_____	_____
13.	w**a**sp	_____	_____
14.	blo**ck**	_____	_____
15.	do**dge**	_____	_____
16.	s**k**i**ll**	_____	_____
17.	tra**y**	_____	_____
18.	fl**ee**	_____	_____

Partial or Complete Phonetic Representation for Spelling

TEXTBOOK REFERENCE
Chapter 9

The young child's use of invented spelling provides considerable insight as to how well the child is learning and internalizing information about the language (Read, 1971). The child applies his or her phonological awareness and acquired knowledge of sounds and patterns to the task of spelling an unfamiliar word. Look at the invented spellings below and decide whether the spellings represent partial or complete phonetic representation. Write *partial* or *complete*.

1. *st* for *seat* _____
2. *kat* for *cat* _____
3. *ct* for *seat* _____
4. *gv* for *give* _____
5. *whl* for *while* _____
6. *jumpt* for *jumped* _____
7. *rede* for *read* _____
8. *yl* for *while* _____
9. *sop* for *soap* _____
10. *plez* for *please* _____
11. *sep* for *step* _____
12. *pik* for *pick* _____
13. *mn* for *man* _____
14. *moshun* for *motion* _____
15. *teme* for *team* _____
16. *cunty* for *country* _____
17. *hav* for *have* _____
18. *samd* for *seemed* _____
19. *batel* for *battle* _____
20. *enuf* for *enough* _____
21. *lafent* for *elephant* _____
22. *selebr8* for *celebrate* _____
23. *site* for *city* _____
24. *split* for *splint* _____
25. *sd* for *said* _____
26. *wun* for *one* _____

Visit http://library.readingteachersnetwork.org/webinars/what-do-they-know-about-words-transitions-childrens-spelling to learn more about spelling development.

 Carreker and Birsh

Five Spelling Rules

A rule word is spelled the way it sounds, but certain information needs to be considered before the word is written. A letter may need to be doubled, dropped, or changed.

Two rules help the speller know when to double a letter in base words:

1. The Rule for Doubling the Final Consonant (the Floss Rule) states that if a one-syllable word ends in /f/, /l/, or /s/ after a short vowel, the final *f*, *l*, or *s* is doubled.
2. The Rule for Doubling the Medial Consonant (the Rabbit Rule) states that if there is one medial consonant sound after a short vowel in a two-syllable word, the medial consonant is doubled.

Three rules help the speller know when to double, drop, or change a letter at the end of a base word before adding a suffix:

1. The Doubling Rule states that if a base word ends in one vowel, one consonant, and one accent, the final consonant is doubled before adding a vowel suffix.
2. The Dropping Rule states that if a base word ends in final *e*, the *e* is dropped before adding a vowel suffix.
3. The Changing Rule states that if a base word ends in one consonant before a final *y*, the *y* is changed to *i* before adding a suffix that does not begin with *i*.

Match the words with the spelling rule that each exemplifies.

1. _____ better
2. _____ omitted
3. _____ thrill
4. _____ happiness
5. _____ determining

a. The Rule for Doubling the Final Consonant (the Floss Rule)
b. The Rule for Doubling a Medial Consonant (the Rabbit Rule)
c. The Doubling Rule
d. The Dropping Rule
e. The Changing Rule

Go to http://library.readingteachersnetwork.org/webinars/five-spelling-rules to view a webinar on the five spelling rules.

Rule Words

For each word listed, write the base word, the suffix, and the spelling rule that is illustrated with each base word or derivative. Use Chapter 9 in Birsh (2011) for reference.

		Base word	Suffix	Rule
1.	hills	_____	_____	_____
2.	letters	_____	_____	_____
3.	swimmer	_____	_____	_____
4.	happiness	_____	_____	_____
5.	racer	_____	_____	_____
6.	dresses	_____	_____	_____
7.	reddish	_____	_____	_____
8.	beginning	_____	_____	_____
9.	penniless	_____	_____	_____
10.	muffins	_____	_____	_____
11.	engaging	_____	_____	_____
12.	omitted	_____	_____	_____
13.	plentiful	_____	_____	_____
14.	enticing	_____	_____	_____
15.	settled	_____	_____	_____
16.	emptied	_____	_____	_____
17.	preferred	_____	_____	_____
18.	permitted	_____	_____	_____

Checkpoints for the Doubling Rule

The Doubling Rule assists students in adding suffixes to base words. When a base word ends in 1) one vowel, 2) one consonant, and 3) one accent, and 4) a vowel suffix is being added, the final consonant is doubled before adding the suffix. If any one of the four checkpoints is missing, the final consonant is not doubled. Look at each base word and the suffix that is to be added. Mark the checkpoints that are present. Write the derivative. If all four checkpoints are present, double the final consonant when writing the derivative.

	One vowel	One consonant	One accent	Vowel suffix	Derivative
hot + est					
run + er					
star + ing					
cup + ful					
steep + est					
stand + ing					
camp + er					
child + ish					
art + ist					
open + er					
begin + er					
benefit + ed					
omit + ed					
travel + ing					
forget + able					

11 Four-Leaf Clover

1. Photocopy the four-leaf clover on page 150 on green card stock and cut the clover apart.
2. Laminate the pieces and affix a magnet to the back of each piece.
3. Place the pieces in random order at the top of a magnetic board.
4. Write the following formulas one at a time on the board.

hot + est =	sip + ed =
run + er =	look + ing =
swim + ing =	slip + er =
shop + ed =	begin + er =
cup + less =	open + ing =
camp + er =	omit + ed =

5. For each formula, students look for the checkpoints for the Doubling Rule (see Activity 72). As students discover each checkpoint, place the pieces of the clover near the formula. If students find all four checkpoints, the final consonant will be doubled. Write the derivative with the doubled final consonant on the board after the equal sign of the appropriate formula. If any one of the checkpoints is missing, the final consonant will not be doubled; write the derivative without the doubled final consonant on the board at the end of the appropriate formula.

Analyzing Words for Spelling

Analyzing words for spelling heightens students' phonemic awareness and orthographic awareness as the students must first determine the sounds in a word and then match the spelling of those sounds in the word. If the sounds are represented by recurring sound–spelling patterns, the word is a regular word. If the sounds are represented by recurring sound–spelling patterns and there is a letter that is doubled, dropped, or changed, the word is a rule word. If the sounds are represented by unexpected orthographic patterns, the word is an irregular word (Carreker, 1992, 2011a).

The words *enough* and *said* are examples of irregular spelling words that contain sound–spelling patterns that are not reliable. Using reliable sound–spelling patterns of the language, one would expect to spell these words *enuf* and *sed*. When reading, one would not be able to sound out the words *enough* and *said*. Therefore, these words are irregular for reading and spelling and must be memorized. However, words that contain less frequent but reliable patterns may be regular for reading but irregular for spelling. For example, in the word *head*, /ĕ/ is spelled *ea*. When the reader encounters this word in reading, he or she will have little difficulty reading the word because a frequent pronunciation of *ea* is /ĕ/. So, the word is regular for reading.

Spelling is a different situation. The most frequent spelling of /ĕ/ is *e*. There is no way to determine when to use *e* and when to use *ea*. The speller must count on frequency. Because *ĕ* is a more frequent spelling, it is the regular, reliable pattern of spelling /ĕ/. Words that contain *ea* to represent /ĕ/ are irregular for spelling although they are regular for reading. Students must memorize these words.

Sort the following words for spelling as regular, rule, or irregular: *batting, pitch, homerun, runner, glove, one, three, nothing, slider, shortstop, player, season, manager, strike, foul*. For each irregular word, underline the part that is irregular.

Regular	Rule	Irregular
_____	_____	_____
_____	_____	_____
_____	_____	_____
_____	_____	_____
_____	_____	_____
_____	_____	_____
_____	_____	_____
_____	_____	_____

Regular, Rule, Irregular for Spelling

Regular words are spelled the way they sound. Regular words do not need to be memorized. *Rule* words are spelled the way they sound, but there is a letter that needs to be doubled, dropped, or changed. Other than the rule that needs to be applied as the words are written, rule words do not need to be memorized. *Irregular* words are spelled in an unexpected way and must be memorized. By analyzing spelling words, students know which words need to be memorized and which ones do not need to be memorized. Analyzing spelling words also calls students' attention to the phonemes and orthographic patterns in words.

Sort the following words as regular, rule, or irregular: *banana, cherry, raspberry, lime, orange, grape, kiwi, strawberry, apple, pineapple, pear, coconut.* For each irregular word, underline the part that is irregular.

Regular	Rule	Irregular
_____	_____	_____
_____	_____	_____
_____	_____	_____
_____	_____	_____

Sort the following words as regular, rule, or irregular: *ocean, sand, swimmer, water, sunning, lifeguard, swordfish, jellyfish, starfish, seaweed, waves, diving.* For each irregular word, underline the part that is irregular.

Regular	Rule	Irregular
_____	_____	_____
_____	_____	_____
_____	_____	_____
_____	_____	_____

Regular or Irregular for Reading and Spelling?

When students understand the orthographic patterns of English, they know how to approach words for reading and spelling. The patterns for reading enable students to translate an orthographic representation into a pronunciation. The patterns for spelling enable students to translate a pronunciation into an orthographic representation. A word that is regular for reading (i.e., an expected pronunciation based on the orthographic pattern) may not be regular for spelling (i.e., an expected orthographic representation based on the pronunciation). Look at the words below. Using your knowledge of orthographic patterns, determine whether the words are regular or irregular for reading and regular or irregular for spelling. The first example is done for you. For reading, the orthographic pattern *spĕnd* produces an expected pronunciation /spĕnd/. For spelling, the pronunciation /spend/ produces the expected orthographic representation, *spend*. Refer to Chapter 9 (Birsh, 2011).

		Reading		Spelling	
		Regular	Irregular	Regular	Irregular
1.	spend	✓		✓	
2.	said				
3.	have				
4.	stroke				
5.	arbor				
6.	weight				
7.	soon				
8.	get				
9.	bus				
10.	relive				

Planning Lessons for Spelling

Use Chapter 9 in Birsh (2011) for reference and plan 5 days of spelling activities.

Spelling

Day 1	Day 2	Day 3	Day 4	Day 5

Morphemes, Origins, Meanings, and Derivatives

Knowledge of morphemes facilitates decoding and provides a springboard for vocabulary development and spelling (Adams, 1990) and bridges the gap between alphabetic reading and comprehension (Foorman & Schatschneider, 1997). Fill in the missing information.

Morpheme	Origin	Meaning	Derivatives
ang	Latin	bend	
astro	Greek	star	
auto	Greek	self, unaided	
bio	Greek		biology, biodegradable, biography
chron		time	chronicle, chronometer, synchronize
cogn	Latin		recognize, cognitive, metacognition
cred	Latin		creed, incredible, credulous
duct		lead	
fer	Latin	bear	
geo	Greek	earth	
logy	Greek		
manu	Latin	hand	
pop	Latin	people	
rupt		break	
trans	Latin	across	
vac	Latin	empty	
vert, vers	Latin	turn	
vis	Latin		vision, visible, invisible

Roots and Combining Forms

Generate derivatives for each of the roots or combining forms.

ject (to throw)
reject

projector

_____

_____

_____

ped (foot)
pedal

pedestrian

_____

_____

_____

spect (to watch)
spectator

inspect

_____

_____

_____

graph (to write, record)
autograph

_____

_____

_____

bio (life)
biographic

_____

_____

_____

ology (study of)
biology

_____

_____

_____

syn, sym (same)
synonym

_____

_____

_____

_____

form (shape)
formation

_____

_____

_____

_____

cur (to go, flow)
current

_____

_____

_____

_____

nom (to name)
nominate

_____

_____

_____

_____

greg (to gather, group)
congregate

_____

_____

_____

_____

voc (to call)
vocation

_____

_____

_____

_____

(continued on next page)

nym (to name)	**pod (foot)**	**cycl (circle)**
antonym	tripod	cyclical

struct (to build)	**vis (to see)**	**meter (measure)**
structure	visit	meter

Visit http://library.readingteachersnetwork.org/lessonets/name-derivative to learn how to play *Name that Derivative.*

Syllables and Morphemes

Syllables are speech units of language that contain one vowel sound, can be represented in written language as words or parts of words, and do not necessarily carry meaning (Moats, 1995). Morphemes are meaning-carrying units of written language such as base words, prefixes, suffixes, roots, and combining forms. Identify the number of syllables and morphemes in each of following words.

		syllables	morphemes			syllables	morphemes
1.	instructor			10.	photographic		
2.	autograph			11.	rattlesnake		
3.	destruction			12.	marker		
4.	salamander			13.	cucumber		
5.	unleaded			14.	barbecue		
6.	waits			15.	manuscript		
7.	interjection			16.	outstanding		
8.	bookkeeper			17.	handshake		
9.	conjunction			18.	bluebonnet		

Syllables and Morphemes

Identify the number of syllables and morphemes in each of the following words.

		syllables	morphemes			syllables	morphemes
1.	population	_____	_____	10.	river	_____	_____
2.	combination	_____	_____	11.	watermelon	_____	_____
3.	mustang	_____	_____	12.	canine	_____	_____
4.	summertime	_____	_____	13.	dressmaker	_____	_____
5.	thermostat	_____	_____	14.	mercury	_____	_____
6.	bumblebee	_____	_____	15.	countryside	_____	_____
7.	protection	_____	_____	16.	computing	_____	_____
8.	wheelbarrow	_____	_____	17.	kangaroo	_____	_____
9.	ambulance	_____	_____	18.	vegetables	_____	_____

12 Word Part Concentration Game

1. Create a concentration game board using the template on page 137.
2. Prepare the game board as an overhead transparency or on an interactive whiteboard.
3. Choose six prefixes, suffixes, and/or roots. (See pages 143–148 for word parts.)
4. Write these word parts randomly in the empty spaces on the game board.
5. Write the meaning of the six word parts randomly in the remaining spaces.
6. Cover each of the spaces with small sticky notes.
7. Place the transparency on the overhead projector if using one.
8. Divide students into teams and determine a rotation.
9. Teams take turns calling out pairs of coordinates (e.g., A3 and B3) to search for a word part and definition that match.
10. Uncover the spaces that correspond to the coordinates.
11. If the word part and its definition match, the team gets a point.
12. If the word part and its definition do not match, cover the two spaces again with the sticky notes.
13. Each team gets only one turn per round, regardless of whether the team has scored a point.
14. The game continues until all of the spaces have been uncovered.

Semantic Word Webs

Semantic webs or maps help children connect related concepts and other semantic relationships to a word (Carreker, 2004). In the web below, students write the new vocabulary word on the line at the top left and the part of speech of the word as it is used in the passage on the line at the top right. Students discuss how the word will function in the passage. For example, if the new word is an adjective, it will describe a noun. In the center circle, students write the origin and definition of the word. In the upper left-hand circle, students write two or three synonyms for the target word. In the upper right-hand circle, students write two or three antonyms. In the lower left-hand circle, students write words that illustrate the function of the word. If the vocabulary word is an adjective, students write a noun in each lower circle that could be described by the new word. If the vocabulary word is a verb, students write an adverb in each of the lower circles that would describe the verb. If the vocabulary word is a noun, students write an adjective in each circle that could describe the word. Finally, on the line below the web, students write a sentence that demonstrates their understanding of the new word.

Web the word *prevaricate.*

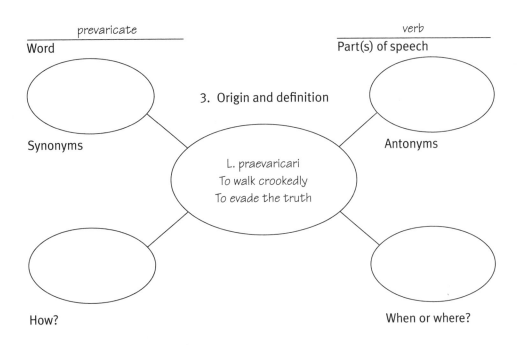

Word _____prevaricate_____   Part(s) of speech _____verb_____

3. Origin and definition

Synonyms   Antonyms

L. praevaricari
To walk crookedly
To evade the truth

How?   When or where?

Sentence

Derivative Webs

A derivative web (Carreker, 2004) is used for words with recognizable, recurring word parts. Students write the new vocabulary word (e.g., *inject*) on the line at the top to the left and the part of speech on the top line at the right. In the center circle, students write the origin, the word parts that make up the word and their meanings, and the definition of the word. In each of the three upper circles, students write a derivative that contains one word part (e.g., three derivatives with prefix *in-* meaning *in* or *into*). In the other three circles, students write three derivatives that contain the other word part (e.g., three derivatives with the root *ject*, meaning *to throw*). Finally, students write a sentence with the word on the line at the bottom of the web. This web is intended to show how learning word parts economizes the learning of new vocabulary and how words with common word parts share a sense of the same meanings.

Web the word *inject*.

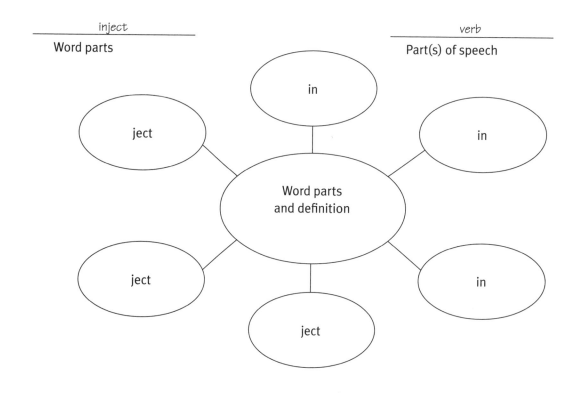

Multiple Meaning Webs

Students use a multiple meaning web (Carreker, 2004) to show multiple meanings of a vocabulary word. They write a word from a passage they are reading on the top left-hand line of the web and in the center circle. Students list possible parts of speech for the word on the top right-hand line. They write six different meanings on the web, one meaning in each circle. Students write a sentence using the meaning that is germane to the passage on the line at the bottom of the web.

Web the word *run*.

run   verb, noun

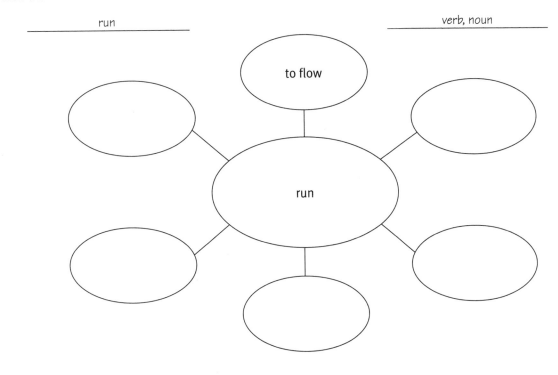

13 Semantic Webs

1. Make photocopies of the semantic web template on page 151.
2. Students create word profiles for the following words and other words that are appropriate. (See Activity 81 for instructions on creating semantic webs.)

meadow	versatile
suburb	semantic
gist	antediluvian
exasperate	

14 Derivative Webs

1. Make photocopies of the derivative web template on page 152.
2. Students create word profiles for the following words and other words that are appropriate. (See Activity 82 for instructions on creating derivative webs.)

telephone	manuscript
bicycle	revert
photograph	transport
tripod	

15 Multiple Meaning Webs

1. Make photocopies of the multiple meaning web on page 152.
2. Students create word profiles for the following words and other words that are appropriate. (See Activity 83 for instructions on creating multiple meaning webs.)

run	lap
slip	hand
tip	give
trunk	

Semantic Feature Analysis

Semantic feature analysis helps students learn new vocabulary and see the relationships among concepts, other words, and ideas or information in a text (Hennessey, 2011). A matrix is constructed that shows examples and features of a targeted concept or word. A check mark signifies a relationship, an *X* signifies a nonrelationship, and a question mark shows uncertainty of a relationship. Without looking at the features across the top of the following matrix, write examples of the target concept in the left-hand column. Mark relationships with check marks, nonrelationships with *X*s, and uncertainty with question marks.

Vegetables	Grows in the ground	Grows on a vine	Is yellow or orange	Contains beta-carotene	Is eatable raw	Is considered a crucifer	Has a high starch content

(continued on next page)

In the following matrix, write the definition of *carnivore* in the first square. Fill in features of carnivores across the top. Write examples of carnivores in the left-hand column. Mark relationships with check marks, nonrelationships with *X*s, and uncertainty with question marks.

Carnivores							

TRY THIS

16 Semantic Feature Analysis

1. Make copies of the template on page 153.
2. Following the process described in Activity 84, have students create semantic feature analysis matrices for the following concepts:

plant	reptile	cities
fruits	mammals	countries
trees	minerals	
animals	transportation	

Thorough knowledge of the phonological, orthographic, and morphological aspects of words builds words in memory, making them easier to retrieve. Thorough knowledge of the semantic, syntactic, and pragmatic uses of words increases students' comprehension. This knowledge also supports fluency as skilled readers use their knowledge of word meanings to group words into meaningful units, which aids prosody. The example below shows a word profile. Such a profile heightens students' awareness of all of the aspects of a word. Study this profile and then create a profile for the word *like*.

Sample Word Profile

Word: light
Number of phonemes: 3   Phonemes: /l/ /ī/ /t/
Rime pattern: ight as in fight, might, tight, sight, bright, plight
Number of letters: 5   Letters: l, i, g, h, t
Number of graphemes: 3   Graphemes: l, igh, t
Spelling pattern(s): irregular for spelling

Origin: Anglo-Saxon

Derivatives: lighter, lightly, lightness, lighten

One definition: a source of brightness

Multiple meanings: not heavy, graceful, sunny, carefree, to ignite

Synonyms: glow, weightless, bright, untroubled, set on fire

Antonyms: heavy, dark, extinguish

Part(s) of speech: noun, adjective, adverb, verb

Usage (formal or informal): Can be used in formal and informal writing

Figurative usages: light as a feather, to make light of, light of my life

(continued on next page)

Word Profile

Word: <u>like</u>

Number of phonemes: _____ Phonemes: _____ _____

Rime pattern: _____

Number of letters: _____ Letters: _____

Number of graphemes: _____ Graphemes: _____

Spelling pattern(s): <u>Medial / ī/ in a one-syllable base word is spelled i-consonant-e</u>_____

Origin: _____

Derivatives: _____

One definition: _____

_____

Multiple meanings: _____

_____

Synonyms: _____

_____

Antonyms: _____

Part(s) of speech: _____

Usage (formal or informal): _____

Figurative usages: _____

ACTIVITY 86

Word Profiles

Create a word profile for the word *play*. Do not use a dictionary. Think about what you know and have learned about all the domains of language—phonology, morphology, syntax, pragmatics, and orthography.

Word Profile

Word: <u>play</u>

Number of phonemes: _____ Phonemes: _____

Rime pattern: _____

Number of letters: _____ Letters: _____

Number of graphemes: _____ Graphemes: _____

Spelling pattern(s): _____

_____

Origin: _____

Derivatives:_____

One definition: _____

_____

Multiple meanings:_____

Synonyms: _____

Antonyms: _____

Part(s) of speech: _____

Usage (formal or informal): _____

Figurative usages: _____

_____

TRY THIS

17 Word Profiles

1. Make copies of the template on page 154.
2. Following the process described in Activities 85 and 86, have students create word profiles for the following words:

tip	trunk	like
top	box	sink
lap	run	rock
slip	light	

Tiers of Vocabulary Words

Hennessy (2011) proposed a three-tiered framework for categorizing:

Tier One words are common basic words that are used in everyday conversations and that most children know; these are not usually the target of instruction.

Tier Two words are more sophisticated words often used by mature language users in speech and writing; found across a variety of texts and domains.

Tier Three words are words with more narrow and specific roles in language; words that are not necessarily familiar to mature language users.

Categorize the following words by tiers. Refer to Chapter 11 (Birsh, 2011).

esophagus	*napkin*	*health*	*euphemism*	*interpret*
hunt	*important*	*rhetoric*	*declare*	*forest*
relate	*erupt*	*dysplasia*	*geriatric*	*knowledge*
protoplasm	*discontent*	*happening*	*featured*	*specific*

Tier One	Tier Two	Tier Three

Student-Friendly Definitions

To introduce new vocabulary words, Beck, McKeown, and Kucan (2008) suggested using student-friendly definitions. These definitions explain the meanings of words in everyday language and provide a familiar context. The definitions are often framed with "someone" or "something" (Hennessy, 2011). Below are vocabulary words and dictionary definitions. The first word is done for you. Create student-friendly definition for the other words. Use Chapter 11 (Birsh, 2011) as a reference.

Word	Dictionary definition	Student-friendly definition
sympathetic[a]	Sympathetic: existing or operating through an affinity, interdependence, or mutual association	*Someone who understands or shares the same feelings or concerns as someone else is sympathetic. For example, even though they are not people, I am sympathetic to abandoned animals who might feel lonely, sad, and afraid.*
vocation[a]	Vocation: a summons or strong inclination to a particular state or course of action	
philosophy[a]	Philosophy: the most basic beliefs, concepts, and attitudes of an individual or group	
inference[a]	Inference: the act of passing from one proposition, statement, or judgment considered as true to another whose truth is believed to follow from that of the former	
exuberant[a]	Exuberant: joyously unrestrained and enthusiastic	

[a]Definitions by permission. From *Merriam Webster's Collegiate® Dictionary, 11th Edition* © 2011 by Merriam-Webster, Incorporated (www.merriam-webster.com).

Precision in Use of Vocabulary

As students learn new words, they will discover that many words share the same or almost the same meaning. The meanings of these words may be similar, but they differ in intensity, making some words more appropriate than other words in a given context. The awareness of intensity helps students understand an author's choice of words and helps them make the best choices for their writing. The words listed below mean *unhappy*. Write *L* for less intensive and *M* for more intensive. Refer to Chapter 11 (Birsh, 2011).

sullen	_____	disconsolate	_____	despondent	_____	sad	_____
gloomy	_____	cheerless	_____	somber	_____	glum	_____
down	_____	distraught	_____	forlorn	_____	sorrowful	_____
devastated	_____	depressed	_____	discontented	_____	blue	_____
disappointed	_____	dejected	_____	low	_____	pessimistic	_____

Usage

Because of the rain, the picnic was canceled, and the children were _____ but not _____ .

The hurricane completely destroyed the town, and the people were not just _____ ;
   they were _____ .

Generate a gradient list of 20 antonyms for *unhappy*.

_____

_____

_____

_____

_____

_____

_____

_____

_____

_____

_____

_____

_____

_____

_____

_____

_____

Comprehension
Summarization

Summarization requires students to think about what they have read and to identify the most important information (Carreker, 2004; Marzola, 2011). Initially, students strive to summarize a passage in about one third the number of words in the passage. Ultimately, students strive to summarize a passage in one quarter the number of words. When students summarize a passage, they must make decisions about what information is important and what information is expendable.

Read the passage called "The Cockroach" on page 156 and write a summary below. This passage has 222 words. A summary with one third the number of words would have 74 words, and a summary with one quarter the number of words would have 55 words.

_____

_____

_____

_____

_____

_____

_____

_____

_____

_____

_____

Visit http://library.readingteachersnetwork.org/webinars/building-background-knowledge-text-sets to learn about building background knowledge with text sets.

Comprehension
Summarization

Read the passage called "The Clydesdale" on page 162 and write a summary below. The passage has 290 words. A summary paragraph with one third the number of words in the passage would have 96 words. A summary paragraph with one quarter the number of words in the passage would have 72 words.

_____

_____

_____

_____

_____

_____

_____

_____

_____

_____

_____

_____

_____

_____

TRY THIS

18 Summarization

1. Photocopy an appropriate passage from pages 155–162.
2. After students have listened to or read the passage, they write a summary paragraph, using one third the number of words in the passage. Serve as a scribe if needed.

Comprehension
Questioning

Answering questions before reading helps students think actively as they read. Answering questions during reading helps students to direct their attention to important sections of the text, monitor their comprehension, and activate fix-up strategies (NRP, 2000). After reading, answering questions confirms that students understand the passage and supports their learning through reading (Carreker, 2004; Marzola, 2005). Care must be taken in crafting a variety of questions. Questions fall into three categories (Pearson & Johnson, 1978):

1. *Text explicit:* The answer to this type of question is easily found in the text.
2. *Text implicit:* The answer to this type of question is suggested in the text.
3. *Script implicit* (or *scriptal*): The answer to this type of question requires the reader's background knowledge rather than information from the text.

Write one of each kind of question about the passage called "The Cockroach" on page 156.

Text explicit

_____

_____

_____

Text implicit

_____

_____

_____

Script implicit (or scriptal)

_____

_____

_____

Write three of each kind of question about the passage called "The Clydesdale" on page 162.

Text explicit

1. _____

_____

2. _____

_____

3. _____

_____

(continued on next page)

Text implicit

1. _____

_____

2. _____

_____

3. _____

_____

Script implicit (or scriptal)

1. _____

_____

2. _____

_____

3. _____

_____

TRY THIS

19 Questioning

1. Copy an appropriate passage on pages 155–162.
2. After students have listened to or read the passage, they generate *text explicit*, *text implicit*, and *script implicit* or *scriptal* (Pearson & Johnson, 1978) questions about the passage. (See Activity 92 for descriptions of these question types.)

Visit http://library.readingteachersnetwork.org/webinars/questions-about-questioning to learn more about questions and questioning.

Parts of Speech

Grammar and syntax aid students in several ways. Students use their knowledge of grammar and syntax to group words into meaningful phrases as they read. This grouping of words gives reading a rhythmic flow (prosody) that facilitates comprehension. Syntactic knowledge helps students understand how to use new vocabulary words in their oral and written discourse. This knowledge helps students construct sentences as they write.

Instruction begins with the key elements of speech—nouns, pronouns, verbs, adjectives, and the articles *the, a,* and *an.* The other parts of speech are added when students have a firm understanding of the essential elements. Prepositions and adverbs expand sentences by telling how, when, or where. Coordinating conjunctions such as *and* and *or* enable students to combine simple sentences into compound sentences. Interjections add emphasis or emotion.

Look at the following sentences. Under each word, write the part of speech that is represented by the word. You can use abbreviations such as *adj.* for *adjective, adv.* for *adverb, conj.* for *conjunction, interj.* for *interjection, prep.* for preposition, and *pron.* for *pronoun.*

1. Three homes at Fifth Street and Pine burned.

2. That dog ran home.

3. The red shirts will run in hot water.

4. Well, I have another run in my sock.

5. Many children happily played a game.

6. The play last night was fun.

7. Those students have no time for fun and games.

8. He left his book on the bus yesterday.

9. No, the teacher said we must finish our assignment.

10. Two big events are planned for this year.

Syntax, the arrangement of sentences, can be introduced or practiced with the use of sentence expansion activities in Chapter 13 (Birsh, 2011). Students begin with a core sentence and add elements to it.

Use the following prompts to expand the sentence *The birds sang*:

1. Write the sentence and add an adjective that describes the birds.

   _____

2. Rewrite the previous sentence and add an adjective and noun that tell what the birds sang.

   _____

3. Rewrite the previous sentence and add a prepositional phrase that tells where the birds sang.

   _____

4. Rewrite the previous sentence, and add another adjective that describes what the birds sang.

   _____

5. Rewrite the previous sentence, and add an adverb or an adverbial phrase that tells when the birds sang.

   _____

Composition
The Descriptive Paragraph

Some students benefit from learning to write paragraphs in sentence form. They write sentences that follow the structure of a paragraph's purpose, edit them, and then write them in paragraph form. As students gain proficiency in vocabulary, syntax, and paragraph writing, this formulaic structure yields to more natural expression. Below are structure sentences for a descriptive paragraph.

1. State the name and category of the object.
2. State the function or use of the object.
3. State a characteristic.
4. State another characteristic.
5. Make a comparison, simile, or metaphor.
6. Restate first sentence, give a fact, or give an opinion.

Using the steps just listed, number these sentences, taken from a descriptive paragraph, in order.

_____ Our world would be a different place without the incredible, versatile spoon.

_____ The spoon is as precious to a chef as a precision jigsaw is to a master craftsman.

_____ One can eat, stir, skim, dip, mold, scoop, dollop, and make rhythmic music with a spoon.

_____ Its half-bulbous bowl is responsible for its adaptability.

_____ The ubiquitous spoon is an amazingly versatile utensil.

_____ Its long, slender handle accounts for its easy maneuverability.

Composition
Writing a Descriptive Paragraph

Look at Figure 5. Write six sentences as prescribed below about the picture in Figure 5.

Figure 5. A picture for writing a descriptive paragraph.

1. State the name and category of the object.

   _____

2. State the function or use of the object.

   _____

3. State a characteristic.

   _____

4. State another characteristic.

   _____

5. Make a comparison or simile.

   _____

6. Restate first sentence, give a fact, or give an opinion.

   _____

(continued on next page)

Edit the sentences.

Write the edited sentences in paragraph form on the lines below.

_____

_____

_____

_____

_____

_____

_____

_____

_____

_____

_____

_____

TRY THIS

20 The Narrative Paragraph

1. Students use the following outline to write a narrative paragraph about the day they discovered a dinosaur in their backyard.

   Sentence 1 – State event.
   Sentence 2 – State what happens first.
   Sentence 3 – State what happens next.
   Sentence 4 – State what happens then.
   Sentence 5 – State what happens finally.
   Sentence 6 – Restate event.

2. Students edit their paragraphs.
3. Students read their paragraphs aloud.

Composition
Writing a Persuasive Paragraph

A persuasive paragraph can be writing using a structure similar to that used for writing a descriptive paragraph. Write six sentences as prescribed below. The topic is *The president should serve one 6-year term*.

1. State your opinion about the topic.

   _____

2. Give a reason for your opinion.

   _____

3. Give an example of that reason.

   _____

4. Give a second reason for your opinion.

   _____

5. Give an example of that reason.

   _____

6. Give your most compelling reason for your opinion.

   _____

7. Give an example of that reason.

   _____

8. Restate your opinion.

   _____

Edit the sentences.

(continued on next page)

Write the edited sentences in paragraph form on the lines below.

_____

_____

_____

_____

_____

_____

_____

_____

_____

_____

_____

_____

_____

_____

_____

Composition
The Painless Paragraph

For students who experience a great deal of difficulty in writing paragraphs, the process can be further simplified with the following procedure.

Look at the picture in Figure 6. List 10 nouns that are seen in the picture in the *Noun* column of the following chart. After listing the nouns, list one verb in present tense that relates to each noun and the picture. After listing the verbs, list two adjectives for each noun.

Adjective	Adjective	Noun	Verb
		sky	
		cowboy	

Figure 6. A picture for writing a painless paragraph.

(continued on next page)

Write 10 sentences, using one row of information from the chart for each sentence. Add an article, a prepositional phrase, a direct object, or an adverb when constructing your sentences.

1. _____
2. _____
3. _____
4. _____
5. _____
6. _____
7. _____
8. _____
9. _____
10. _____

Edit your sentences. Delete one of the two adjectives that describe each noun. Rearrange words. Insert a word. Are there sentences that could be combined into a complex sentence?

_____
_____
_____
_____
_____
_____
_____
_____
_____
_____
_____

Choose six edited sentences. Write them in order below in paragraph form.

_____
_____
_____
_____
_____
_____
_____
_____
_____
_____
_____
_____

Composition
Transition Words and Phrases

TEXTBOOK REFERENCE
Chapter 13

The flow of writing is facilitated by the use of transition words (Hochman, 2011). Transition words sequence ideas, emphasize a point, indicate a change in thought, illustrate a point, or draw a thought or idea to a conclusion. Categorize these transitional words: *first, finally, therefore, for example, obviously, yet, above all, before, specifically, thus, in summary, as an illustration, otherwise, certainly, keep in mind*

Time and sequence

_____

_____

_____

Emphasis

_____

_____

_____

Change of direction

_____

_____

_____

Illustration

_____

_____

_____

Conclusion

_____

_____

_____

Final *e* at the end of words is almost always silent. Final *e* serves several functions (Wilson, 2011). It is used to make a vowel long or to make *c* or *g* soft. It can be part of a consonant-*le* syllable. Because English words do not end in *v*, *e* is added as the final letter when a word ends in final /v/, and it may or may not influence the vowel sound. In the chart are base words that end in silent *e*. Write in the reason for the final silent *e*, and then form derivatives by adding the indicated endings and suffixes. Use Chapter 16 in Birsh (2011) for reference.

Word	Reason for silent *e*	Derivatives
name		(Add *-ing*, *-ed*, and *-less*.)
shave		(Add *-ing*, *-ed*, and *-er*.)
battle		(Add *-ing*, *-ed*, and *-ment*.)
infringe		(Add *-ing*, *-er*, and *-ment*.)
trace		(Add *-ing*, *-ed*, and *-able*.)

Chart from Wilson, B. (2011). Instruction for older students with a word-level reading disability. In J.R. Birsh (Ed.), *Multisensory teaching of basic language skills* (3rd ed., p. 489). Baltimore: Paul H. Brookes Publishing Co.; adapted by permission.

Terms for Assessment

Match each term with the correct definition. Use Chapter 14 in Birsh (2011) for reference.

1. _____ norm-referenced test

2. _____ criterion-referenced test

3. _____ curriculum-referenced test

4. _____ screening

5. _____ progress monitoring

6. _____ diagnostic measure

7. _____ outcome measure

8. _____ formal assessment

9. _____ informal assessment

10. _____ pseudowords

11. _____ formative data

12. _____ summative data

13. _____ DIBELS

14. _____ TPRI

15. _____ PALS

a. Dynamic Indicators of Basic Literacy Skills (Good & Kiminski, 2002).

b. periodic assessment that measures progress in response to specific instruction

c. Texas Primary Reading Inventory (University of Texas System and Texas Education Agency, 2006).

d. Brief assessment that identifies students who may need additional or alternate forms of instruction

e. Assessment that measures knowledge attained and knowledge yet to be acquired in a domain

f. Nonsense words that are phonetically regular

g. Standardized assessment that must be administered and scored according to prescribed procedures

h. Phonological Awareness Literacy Screening (Invernizzi, Meier, & Juel, 2002).

i. Data that provide information about knowledge to be applied to long-term, comprehensive goals

j. Data that provide information about knowledge to be applied to short-term goals

k. Assessment that measures knowledge that has been taught

l. Assessment that classifies a student in terms of achievement or improvement of grade-level performance

m. Assessment that provides a detailed analysis of a student's strengths and weaknesses

n. Assessment that measures performance in relation to a norm cohort or group

o. Assessments that are not standardized

Terms for Planning of Lessons, Adolescent Literacy, and Older Students

Match each term with its correct definition. Use Chapters 15 and 17 in Birsh (2011) for reference.

1. _____ active listening

2. _____ structured instruction

3. _____ direct instruction

4. _____ diagnostic teaching

5. _____ prescriptive teaching

6. _____ systematic and cumulative instruction

a. Instruction in which concepts are explicitly taught
b. Teaching that is informed by a continual assessment of student needs
c. Teaching with a logical order of introduction of concepts that progress from easiest to more difficult
d. Instruction that follows ordered procedures
e. Giving one's full attention to the speaker and making eye contact with him or her
f. Individualized teaching based on needs

Creating an
Educational Memories Sample

TEXTBOOK REFERENCE
Chapter 19

An educational memories sample (Blumenthal, 1981) records a person's positive and negative memories of his or her educational experience. It can reveal insights that a person has about his or her strengthens and difficulties, how the person has dealt with any difficulties, and the emotional impact of the difficulties. It also provides a writing sample that demonstrates the person's organizational and writing skills. People without learning problems tend to have more positive memories of their educational experiences than those with learning problems (Blumenthal, 2011).

On the lines below, write your memories of your educational experiences.

_____

_____

_____

_____

_____

_____

_____

_____

_____

_____

_____

_____

_____

_____

_____

_____

_____

_____

_____

_____

_____

_____

_____

Spanish Phonemes

There are 23 phonemes or speech sounds in Spanish (Barrutia & Schwegler, 2004). In English, there are about 44. Many sounds in Spanish and English directly transfer from one language to the other (Cárdenas-Hagan, 2011). These sounds are *cognates*.

Look at the English sounds below. Check *yes* if there is a cognate in Spanish. Check *no* if there is no cognate. Use Chapter 20 in Birsh (2011) for reference.

Cognate in Spanish?

English consonant sound	Yes	No
/m/	_____	_____
/s/	_____	_____
/sh/	_____	_____
/t/	_____	_____
/d/	_____	_____
/j/	_____	_____
/zh/	_____	_____
/k/	_____	_____
/th/	_____	_____

Look at the Spanish sounds below. Check *yes* if there is a cognate in English. Check *no* if there is no cognate.

Cognate in English?

Spanish consonant sound	Yes	No
/rr/	_____	_____
/b/	_____	_____
/ñ/	_____	_____
/p/	_____	_____
/g/	_____	_____
/f/	_____	_____
/ch/	_____	_____
/l/	_____	_____

Terms for Executive Function and Learning Strategies, Adolescent Literacy, Multisensory Mathematics Instruction, Assistive Technology, and the Law

TEXTBOOK REFERENCE
Chapters 17, 18, 21, and 22

Match each term with the correct definition. Use Chapters 17, 18, 21, 22, and 23 in Birsh (2011) for reference.

1. _____ Skills for Organizing and Reading Efficiently (SkORE)
2. _____ quick tricks
3. _____ cloze technique
4. _____ executive function
5. _____ mind map
6. _____ addend
7. _____ adolescent literacy
8. _____ regrouping
9. _____ multiplier
10. _____ multiplicand
11. _____ dividend
12. _____ division radical
13. _____ divisor
14. _____ assistive technology
15. _____ continuous speech recognition
16. _____ Individuals with Disabilities Education Act (IDEA)
17. _____ attention deficit-hyperactivity
18. _____ Americans with Disabilities Act (ADA)
19. _____ individualized education program (IEP)
20. _____ due process
21. _____ dyslexia

a. A graphic organizer that connects ideas
b. A number to added to another
c. A mathematical symbol used for division facts ($\div$)
d. The number that tells how many times a certain number is to be produced
e. A new term for *carrying* and *borrowing*
f. A study skills system designed to help students achieve the goals of self-awareness, self-management, and self-advocacy
g. A fill-in-the-blank technique
h. A total amount that is to be divided by another number
i. The number that a total number is divided by
j. Core components are goal setting, planning, organization of behaviors over time, flexibility, attention and memory systems, and self-regulation
k. Strategies that improve students' attention, cooperation, memory, and organization and reduce common errors
l. Reading instruction focused on Grades 4 through 12
m. The number that states the size that is to be multiplied
n. Pertains to voice recognition software that allows the speaker to speak at a conversational pace (rather than saying each word separately)
o. Federal law that protects the rights of people with disabilities

(continued on next page)

p. A document that identifies a child as having a disability and delineates referral, evaluation, special education, and related services to be provided

q. The rights of the parents of a child with disorder disabilities to receive notice of changes in the child's education program and a hearing if there is a disagreement

r. A specific learning disability characterized by difficulties with accurate and/or fluent word recognition and by poor spelling and decoding abilities

s. Disorder characterized by difficulty attending to and completing tasks

t. Equipment or products used by individuals with disabilities to improve functioning in activities

u. Federal legislation that requires special education and related services for qualified students with disabilities

21 Fraction Lotto Game

By Margaret B. Stern (author of "Multisensory Mathematics Instruction," Chapter 21 in Birsh, 2011)

1. Make two photocopies of the Fraction Lotto Template on page 163 on white cardstock. These are the game boards.
2. Photocopy two additional copies of the Fraction Lotto Template on green card stock and cut the pieces apart. You will have 60 green cards.
3. Make four piles of like sizes of the green cards: 1 whole, $\frac{1}{2}$, $\frac{1}{4}$, $\frac{1}{8}$.
4. Make a denominator deck. On 24 uncut 3" × 5" white index cards, write fractions with the following denominators and the numerators left blank:

$$\frac{}{2}\ \frac{}{2}\ \frac{}{4}\ \frac{}{4}\ \frac{}{4}\ \frac{}{4}\ \frac{}{8}\ \frac{}{8}\ \frac{}{8}\ \frac{}{8}\ \frac{}{8}\ \frac{}{8}$$

$$\frac{}{2}\ \frac{}{2}\ \frac{}{4}\ \frac{}{4}\ \frac{}{4}\ \frac{}{4}\ \frac{}{8}\ \frac{}{8}\ \frac{}{8}\ \frac{}{8}\ \frac{}{8}\ \frac{}{8}$$

5. Make a numerator deck. Cut 24 3 × 5 index cards in half and write one of the following numerators on each piece: 1, 2, and 3. Make eight of each numerator card.
6. Students are arranged on two teams, with one game board for each team.
7. The four piles of the green cards that have been sorted by size are placed face up on the playing surface.
8. Place the shuffled denominator deck face down on the playing surface and the shuffled numerator deck face down on the playing surface.
9. The first player on one team draws a card from the denominator deck and names the denominator (e.g., "I got eighths").
10. The player then draws from the numerator deck and names the numerator and the fraction that is represented with the two cards: "Two! I now have two eighths."
11. The player adds two green eighth cards to the team's game board.
12. The other team takes a turn and the game continues until one team covers its board with green cards.
13. Students can exchange equivalent smaller pieces for one larger piece: "I'll exchange four eighths for one half" or "I'll exchange two halves for one whole."
14. A team can pass if the fraction created by the numerator and denominator cards that it has drawn is too large for the team's remaining spaces.

From Stern, M., & Gould, T. (1992). *Structural arithmetic III teachers' guide* (p. 104). Cambridge, MA: Educators Publishing Service; used by permission of Educators Publishing Service, 625 Mt. Auburn Street, Cambridge, MA, 800-225-5750, http://www.epsbooks.com

ACTIVITY 106

Planning 5 Days of Lessons

Use the lesson plan template on the following pages to plan a week of complete intermediate lessons. Different curricula have different orders of presentation. The order of presentation is not as important as the principles of systematic instruction. The key considerations in planning lessons are what concepts have been previously introduced and what concepts need to be presented and in what order. For purposes of this activity, the following is assumed:

- Students have been introduced to the most frequent sounds of the consonants.
- Students have been introduced to the letter clusters *ck, ng, th* (both voiced and unvoiced), *sh*, and *ch*.
- All of the short and long vowel sounds have been introduced and practiced, and students have learned *oo* as in *book* and *ee*.
- The closed, open, vowel-consonant-*e*, and consonant-*le* syllable types have been introduced and practiced.
- Students have been introduced to the VCCV syllable division pattern.
- Students have been introduced to suffixes *-s, -ed, -ing, -es, -ness,* and *-less*.
- Students have been introduced to the Floss Rule, the Rabbit Rule, and the Doubling Rule.
- Students are able to name all letters of the alphabet accurately and quickly.
- Students have been introduced to the vowel-*r* pattern *er* and are ready to learn the other vowel-*r* patterns.

When filling in the lesson plan template, determine and list the following:

- The new concepts for introduction
- The sounds to be reviewed daily for reading and spelling
- Words that can be used each day for single-word practice and spelling
- Sentences that can be used each day for practice
- Irregular words that will need to be introduced or reviewed

Use the following while planning activities:

- Use the passages in Figure 3 and pages 155-162 to plan passage reading practice.
- Use the passages in Figure 3 and pages 155-162 to plan fluency and/or prosody activities.
- Use the passages in Figure 3 and pages 155-162 to plan vocabulary and comprehension activities.
- Use Figure 15.2 in Birsh (2011) as a reference.
- Use the chapters in Birsh (2011) for information and ideas.

Appendix P is available as a checklist for classroom organization and management to maximize the instruction (Schedler & Bitler, 2004).

(continued on next page)

Activities	Day 1	Day 2
Alphabet and dictionary, phonological awareness, and morphology study	Phonological awareness	Alphabet and dictionary
Reading decks	Reading, spelling, and affix decks are reviewed.	Reading, spelling, and affix decks are reviewed.
Spelling deck		
Multisensory introduction of letter or concept		
Reading practice		
Spelling		
Handwriting (does not occur every lesson)		
Extended reading and writing		
Comprehension and listening strategies		
Oral language practice and composition	Review nouns, verbs, and adjectives. Students identify parts of speech in the reading practice sentences.	Introduce prepositions. Students write five sentences with prepositional phrases.

(continued on next page)

Day 3	Day 4	Day 5
Morphology study: words of Latin origin	Morphology study: words of Latin origin	Alphabet and dictionary
Reading, spelling, and affix decks are reviewed.	Reading, spelling, and affix decks are reviewed.	Reading, spelling, and affix decks are reviewed.

From Birsh, J.R., & Schedler, J.-F. (2011). Planning multisensory structured language lessons and the classroom environment. In J.R. Birsh (Ed.), *Multisensory teaching of basic language skills* (3rd ed., p. 461). Baltimore: Paul H. Brookes Publishing Co; adapted by permission.

(*Sources:* Cox, 1984; Neuhaus Education Center, 2000.)

Appendix Contents

PHOTOCOPIABLE MATERIAL

Major Research Findings on Reading

ORAL LANGUAGE

Long before children begin to read, they need language and literacy experiences at home and in pre-school to develop a wide range of knowledge that will support them later in acquiring linguistic skills necessary for reading. These include language play such as saying rhymes, writing messages, listening to and examining books, developing oral vocabulary and verbal reasoning, and learning the purposes of reading. Exposure to reading aloud and oral language play foster development of phonemic awareness.

PHONEMIC AWARENESS

Reading development depends on the acquisition of phonemic awareness and other phonological processes. Phonemic awareness is the ability to understand the sound structure in spoken words. To learn to read, however, children must also be able to pay attention to the sequence of sounds or phonemes in words and to manipulate them. This is difficult because of the coarticulation of the separate sounds in spoken words. Children learn to do this by engaging in intensive oral language activities of sufficient duration, such as identifying and making rhymes, counting and working with syllables in words, segmenting initial and final phonemes, hearing and blending sounds, analyzing initial and final sounds of words, and segmenting words fully before learning to read and during beginning reading. This training facilitates and predicts later reading and spelling achievement.

ALPHABET KNOWLEDGE

It is essential that children learn the alphabet and be able to say the names of the letters, recognize the shapes, and write the letters. These skills are powerful predictors of reading success.

PHONICS

Along with instruction on letter names, children need well-designed and focused phonics instruction to learn letter–sound correspondences. Fast and efficient decoding and word-reading skills rest on this alphabetic principle: how the written spellings of words systematically represent the phonemes in the spoken words. The beginning reader must begin to connect the 26 letters of the alphabet with the approximately 44 phonemes in English.

PRACTICE WITH DECODABLE TEXTS

Children need to practice new sounds and letters using materials (i.e., controlled decodable texts) that directly reinforce the new information and that review what children already know for maximum gains in fluency and automaticity.

(continued on next page)

Sources: Adams (1990); Center for the Improvement of Early Reading Achievement (1998); Lyon (1999); Torgesen (2004).
Multisensory Teaching of Basic Language Skills Activity Book, Revised Edition, by Suzanne Carreker and Judith R. Birsh

EXPOSURE TO SIGHT WORDS AND IRREGULAR WORDS

Sight word reading happens when children are able to read words from memory. Repeated exposures build the alphabetic features in memory so words can be read by sight.

It is also important for children to have a store of high-frequency irregularly spelled words so that they can read more than just controlled texts when they are ready.

ACCURATE AND AUTOMATIC WORD RECOGNITION

Fluency and comprehension depend on accurate and automatic word recognition. Slow decoders are poor at comprehension because of reduced attentional and memory resources. Systematic word recognition instruction on common, consistent letter–sound relationships and syllable patterns supports successful word recognition skills.

SPELLING

When children are familiar with the spelling regularities of English, their reading and spelling are strengthened. Opportunities to apply the predictable and logical rules and spelling patterns that match the reading patterns being learned give children a double immersion in the information. Spelling is an essential and interconnected complement to reading instruction.

COMPREHENSION

Comprehension depends on the activation of relevant background knowledge and is related strongly to oral language comprehension and vocabulary growth. Along with explicit vocabulary instruction, metacognitive strategies such as questioning, predicting, making inferences, clarifying misunderstandings, and summarizing while reading should be included in comprehension instruction.

SYSTEMATIC, EXPLICIT INSTRUCTION

Poor readers need highly systematic, structured, explicit, and intensive one-to-one or small-group instruction that recognizes their developmental level in phonemic awareness, word recognition, and comprehension processes. Implicit instruction has been found to be counterproductive with children with learning disabilities or children at risk for not learning to read and produces fewer gains in word recognition and decoding skills than does explicit, intensive instruction based on systematic phonics.

WELL-TRAINED TEACHERS

Well-trained, accomplished teachers who can analyze instruction and monitor progress, set goals, and continue to learn about effective practices are the mainstay of children's success in learning to read.

Sources: Adams (1990); Center for the Improvement of Early Reading Achievement (1998); Lyon (1999); Torgesen (2004).
Multisensory Teaching of Basic Language Skills Activity Book, Revised Edition, by Suzanne Carreker and Judith R. Birsh

Instant Letter Recognition Chart

Dictionary Relay

Target word	Quartile	Page #	Column #

Concentration Game Board

	1	2	3	4
A				
B				
C				

Six Syllable Types

Closed	Open	Vowel-consonant-*e*	Vowel-*r*	Vowel pair	Final stable syllable

Words for Six Syllable Types Chart

and	got	cub	fast	run	met	send	hen
him	not	get	plant	splint	clock	strand	blank
he	she	go	hi	so	no	me	be
five	cake	rope	cube	these	cape	line	note
seem	look	need	paint	boat	each	spoon	spoil
first	fern	fork	far	fur	third	mark	short
candle	scramble	uncle	noodle	steeple	bottle	ruffle	puzzle
nation	nature	mention	adventure	explosion	invention	erosion	capture

(continued on next page)

Words for Six Syllable Types Chart

end	top	tub	list	gum	hand	sent
milk	hot	hunt	split	slant	block	shrank
locate	baby	lilac	sofa	fever	noble	belong
strike	flake	smoke	tune	theme	scrape	choke
sheet	good	cream	paid	float	peach	shout
thirst	herd	shark	spark	spur	bird	born
handle	ramble	ankle	needle	poodle	battle	raffle
lotion	picture	motion	mixture	abrasion	intention	emotion
					leg	nurture

Practice Words for Syllable Division

VCCV SYLLABLE DIVISION PATTERN

VC´ V (first choice): Divide between the consonants; accent first syllable.

All closed syllables
basket, bullet, cactus, campus, candid, catnip, classic, coffin, combat, common, conduct, custom, distant, distinct, fabric, format, gallop, gambit, goblin, gospel, happen, helmet, hemlock, insect, insult, kitten, mascot, mitten, napkin, pencil, public, rabbit, rustic, subject, sudden, tonsil, tunnel

Mixed syllables
after, better, bitter, bladder, butter, center, chapter, charter, chimney, cluster, coffee, comfort, comma, corner, costume, curtail, darling, dinner, doctor, donkey, elbow, elder, expert, factor, fancy, fellow, fifty, finger, fortune, furnish, garment, German, glitter, grammar, gutter, hammer, happy, hunger, ladder, luster, market, mellow, member, nectar, parlor, penny, pepper, perfect, plaster, puppy, scarlet, slender, supper, yellow

VC CV´ (second choice): Divide between the consonants; accent the second syllable.

All closed syllables
abduct, affect, collect, command, commit, compel, concrete, conduct, connect, consist, consult, contempt, discuss, enlist, enrich, extinct, inject, insist, intend, pastel, upset

Mixed syllables
absorb, canteen, cartoon, combine, compete, complain, compose, compute, condone, confess, confide, confuse, display, distort, endorse, engage, entire, escape, estate, esteem, invade, perhaps

V´ CCV (third choice): Divide before the first consonant; accent the first syllable.

All open and closed syllables
April, apron, fragrant, macron, secret

VCV SYLLABLE DIVISION PATTERN

V´ CV (first choice): Divide before the consonant; accent the first syllable.

All open and closed syllables
basic, basis, bogus, caper, climax, evil, final, iris, lilac, lotus, nomad, open, raven, robot, silent, sinus, total, totem, tulip, unit, zero

Mixed syllables
baby, decoy, duty, even, favor, fever, fiber, gravy, locate, navy, paper, prelude, rotate, ruby, silent, spider, super, vacate

V´ CV (second choice): Divide before the consonant; accent the second syllable.

All open and closed syllables
beyond, deduct, deflect, depend, depress, divine, lament

(continued on next page)

(*Note:* In an open, unaccented syllable, *a* is pronounced /ŭ/ as in *parade* and *i* is pronounced /ĭ/ as in *divide*.)

Mixed syllables
crusade, decline, deduce, degree, deny, deport, elope, elude, evoke, promote, result, unite

VC´ V (third choice): Divide after the consonant; accent the first syllable.

cabin, camel, city, civil, clinic, copy, devil, ever, exile, exit, gravel, habit, legend, level, limit, livid, medal, melon, metal, modern, panel, river, robin, salad, second, seven, toxic, travel, value, venom

VCCCV SYLLABLE DIVISION PATTERN

VC´ CCV (first choice): Divide after the first consonant; accent the first syllable.

children, dandruff, escrow, fortress, hamster, hundred, monster, ostrich, pantry, pilgrim, spectrum

VC CCV´ (second choice): Divide after the first consonant; accent the second syllable.

complete, destroy, distract, emblaze, employ, enclose, exclaim, exclude, explain, exploit, extract, extreme, surprise

V´CC CV (third choice): Divide after the second consonant; accent the first syllable.

bankrupt, muskrat, partner, pumpkin, sandwich

VV SYLLABLE DIVISION PATTERN

V´ V (first choice): Divide between the vowels; accent first syllable.

bias, lion, neon, triumph, truant

V´ V (second choice): Divide between the vowels that could but do not form a digraph or a diphthong; accent first syllable.

boa, diet, poem, quiet, stoic

V V´ (third choice): Divide between the vowels; accent the second syllable.

coerce, create, duet

WORDS WITH THREE OR MORE SYLLABLES TO USE FOR SYLLABLE DIVISION PRACTICE

alfalfa, Atlantic, assemble, basketball, butterfly, carpenter, chinchilla, contradict, controvert, conundrum, cornerstone, counterpart, cucumber, cumulus, dependent, dislocate, elastic, electromagnet, electromotor, encounter, entertain, establish, fantastic, formula, fundamental, gorilla, identify, identity, improvise, independent, insulate, intellect, introduce, investment, justify, membership, nocturnal, particular, peppercorn, peppermint, permeate, porcupine, principle, reinforce, reluctant, republic, resemble, testament, unicorn, vanilla

Suffixes, Prefixes, Roots, and Combining Forms

SUFFIXES

A suffix is a letter or group of letters added to the end of a base word, root, or combining form, to change its form, usage, tense, or meaning.

-able	able to
-al	related to
-ed	past tense
-en	made of
-er	more
-er	one who or that which
-es	more than one
-est	the most
-ful	full of
-ible	able to
-ic	having characteristics of
-ing	happening now
-ish	quality of
-ity	state of
-less	without
-ly	quality of
-ment	state of
-ness	state of
-or	more
-or	one who or that which
-ous	full of
-s	more than one
-y	quality of

PREFIXES

A prefix is a letter or letters added to the beginning of a base word, root, or combining form to change its meaning.

ab-	away from
ad- (ac-, af- ag-, al-, an-, ar-, as-, at-)	to, toward
auto-	self, unaided
be-	to cause, become
bene-	good
bi-	two

(continued on next page)

 143

circum-	around
con- (co-, com-, cor-)	with, together
contra-	against
counter-	against, in opposition
de-	down, away from
dec-	ten
demi-	half
dis-	the reverse of
dys-	not normal
en- (em-)	to cause, provide
ex-	out of, away from
extra-	outside, beyond
fore-	previously, in front of
hydro-	water
hyper-	extra, beyond, over
hypo-	under, below
in- (il-, im-, ir-)	in, on, toward
in-	not
inter-	between
intra-	inside
micro-	small
mid-	middle
mini-	small
mis-	wrongly, badly
mono-	one, single
non-	not, against
nona-	nine
ob- (oc-, of-, op-)	in the way of
octa-	eight
omni-	all, general
poly-	many
post-	after
pre-	before
pseudo-	false, pretend
quadr-, quar-	four
quint-	five
re-	back, again
retro-	backward
self-	by oneself
semi-	half
sept-	seven
sext-	six
super-	above
trans-	across
tri-	three
ultra-	beyond
un-	not
under-	below, beneath

(continued on next page)

uni-	one
up-	upper
vice-	in place of

ROOTS (LATIN) AND COMBINING FORMS (GREEK)

aero	Greek air
agri	Latin field
alter	Latin other
ambi	Latin both
ambul	Latin walk
amo	Latin love
andr, anthr	Greek mankind
ang	Latin bend
anim	Latin life, spirit, soul
anni, annu, enni	Latin year
anthropo	Greek human
apt, ept	Latin fasten
aqua	Latin water
arch, archy	Greek ruler, to rule
aristo	Greek best
art	Latin skill
astro	Greek star
atmo	Greek vapor
audi	Latin hear
auto	Greek self
belli	Latin war
biblio	Greek books
bio	Greek life
brev	Latin short
cad, cas, cid	Latin fall or befall
camp	Latin field
capit, capt	Latin head, chief
cardi	Greek heart
caus, cus	Latin cause, motive
cede, ceed, cess	Latin go, yield, surrender
centr	Latin center
cepha	Greek head
cept, cap, ceiv, ceit	Latin seize, take, catch
cern, cert	Latin separate, decide
cess	Latin go, move
chloro	Greek pale green
chromo	Greek color
chrono	Greek time
cide, cise	Latin cut, kill
claim, clam	Latin shout
clar	Latin clear
cogn	Latin know

(continued on next page)

corp	Latin body
cosmo	Greek universe
crat, cracy	Greek rule
cred	Latin belief
cur, curs, cours	Latin run, go
cycl	Greek circle
demo	Greek people
dent	Latin tooth
derm	Greek skin
dex	Latin right
dic, dict	Latin speak
div	Latin separate
drome	Greek run
duc, duce, duct	Latin lead
dyn, dynamo	Greek power, force
eco	Greek house, home
ecto	Greek outside
ego	Latin self
endo	Greek within
eques, equi	Latin horse
fac, fic, fact, fect	Latin make
fer	Latin bring, bear, yield
flect, flex	Latin bend
form	Latin shape
gen	Greek birth
geo	Greek earth
gon	Greek angle
grad	Latin step, degree, walk
graph, gram	Greek write, record
grat, gre	Latin pleasing
greg	Latin gather, group
hal	Latin breathe
helio	Greek sun
hema, hemo	Greek blood
homo	Latin alike
hydr, hydra	Greek water
hypn, hypno	Greek sleep
ideo	Greek idea
ject	Latin throw
jud, jur, jus	Latin law, judge
junct	Latin join
kin, kine, cine	Greek move
lat	Latin side or wide
lect, leg, lig	Latin choose, read, speak
leg	Latin law
liber	Latin free
lith, litho	Greek stone
loc, loqu	Latin speak, talk, say

(continued on next page)

loco	Latin place
logo, (o)logy	Greek word, study of
luc, luna, lumin	Latin light
man, manu	Latin hand
mania	Greek madness, obsession
mar	Latin sea
mech	Greek machine
memo	Latin to bring to mind
meter, metr	Greek measure
mis, mit	Latin send
mob, mot, mov	Latin move
mod	Latin measure
moni	Latin warn
morph, morphe	Greek form
mort	Latin death
myo	Greek muscle
nat	Latin born
naut, naus	Greek sailor, ship
nav	Latin ship
neo	Greek new
nom	Latin name
noun	Latin declare
nov	Latin new
nym	Greek name
ortho	Greek straight, correct
pan, panto	Greek all
path	Greek feeling
ped	Greek child
ped	Latin foot
pel, puls	Latin drive, push
phila, philo	Greek love, affinity for
phobia	Greek irrational fear, hate
phono	Greek sound
photo	Greek light
phyll	Greek leaves
phys	Greek nature
plic, ply	Latin fold
pneumo	Greek breath, lung
pod	Greek foot
pol, poli, polis	Greek city
pon, pos, pose, pound	Latin put, place
pop	Latin people
port	Latin carry
psych	Greek mind
pulmo	Latin lung
pup	Latin child, doll
put, pute	Latin think
ras, raz	Latin scrape

(continued on next page)

rect	Latin lead straight
rupt	Latin break
san	Latin health
sanct	Latin holy
saur	Greek lizard, serpent
scope	Greek see, watch
scribe, script	Latin write, written
sect	Latin cut
sequi	Latin follow
sist, sta, stat	Latin stand, endure
soph	Greek wisdom, cleverness
spec, spect	Latin see, watch
sphere	Latin circle
spir	Latin breath, breathe
stereo	Greek solid, firm
stru, struct	Latin build
syn, sym	Greek same
tact, tag, tang, tig	Latin touch
techn	Greek art, craft
ten, tend, tain, tin, tinu	Latin have, hold
tend, tens, tent	Latin stretch
theo	Greek God
therm	Greek heat
tort	Latin twist
tract	Latin pull
vac	Latin empty
ven, veni, vent	Latin come
ver, veri	Latin true, genuine
vert, vers	Latin turn
vid, vis	Latin see
vit, vita, viv, vivi	Latin to live
voc, vok, voke	Latin call

Rapid Word-Recognition Chart

Source: Carreker (2011a).
Multisensory Teaching of Basic Language Skills Activity Book, Revised Edition, by Suzanne Carreker and Judith R. Birsh

Four-Leaf Clover

The four large pieces represent the four checkpoints of the Doubling Rule: one vowel (1V), one consonant (1C), one accent (1'), and a vowel suffix (V in a box). The pieces are placed together to make a four-leaf clover. If all checkpoints are present, the fifth piece (the stem) is added, signifying that the final consonant of the base word or root is doubled. See Try This 11 for directions on how to make the four-leaf clover.

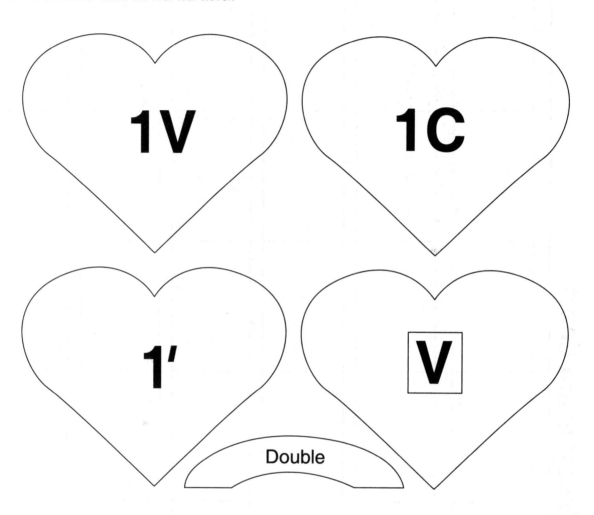

Word Webs

Semantic Web

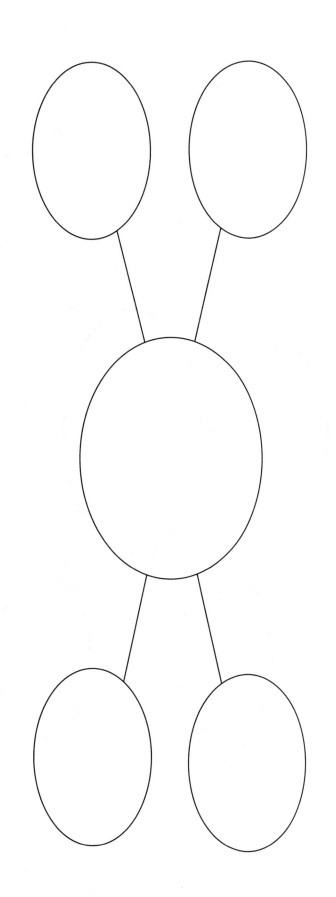

Derivative or Multiple Meaning Web

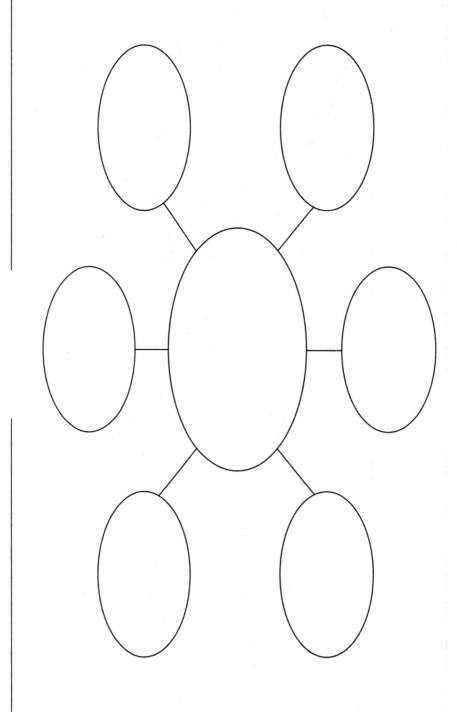

Semantic Feature Analysis

Key: √ = a relationship; X = a nonrelationship; ? = unsure of a relationship.

Word Profile

Word: _____

Number of phonemes: _____   Phonemes: _____

Rime pattern: _____

Number of letters: _____   Letters: _____

Number of graphemes: _____   Graphemes: _____

Spelling pattern (Is there a regular pattern or rule, or is the word irregular?):

_____

_____

Origin: _____

Derivatives: _____

_____

One definition: _____

_____

Multiple meanings: _____

_____

_____

Synonyms: _____

_____

Antonyms: _____

_____

Part(s) of speech: _____

Usage (formal or informal): _____

Figurative usages: _____

_____

Frog Facts

A frog is not a mammal or a reptile. It is an amphibian. An amphibian spends part of its life in the water and part of its life on land. A frog begins its life in the water. When an egg hatches, it becomes a tadpole that stays in the water for a time. The tadpole then becomes a frog and spends most of its life on land.

A frog has big, strong hind legs. With its powerful hind legs, it can jump 20 times its length. A frog breathes by means of lungs and through its skin. It has a thin membrane at the bottom of its eyelid. This is how a frog closed its eyes. A frog is cold-blooded and must hibernate in the winter.

A frog helps humans by eating insects. Some people think that frogs' legs are a treat to eat. Some people use them for fishing bait.

152 words

(continued on next page)

From Neuhaus Education Center. (1998). *Basic language skills: Concept manual, book two* (p. 63). Bellaire, TX: Author; adapted by permission.
Copyright © 1998 by Neuhaus Education Center. All rights reserved. In *Multisensory Teaching of Basic Language Skills Activity Book, Revised Edition* by Suzanne Carreker and Judith R. Birsh (2011, Paul H. Brookes Publishing Co., Inc.)
 155

The Cockroach

It makes you squirm. It makes you shudder. It has enjoyed life for thousands and thousands of years. There are over a thousand kinds of it found all over the world. It is closely related to the cricket and the grasshopper but is not as pleasing. It is, in fact, the most disgusting of all insects. What is it? It is the annoying cockroach.

The cockroach has an oval-shaped body that is covered with a shiny, tough casing. It has two long feelers. It has long legs that are covered with bristles. These legs are strong and help the cockroach to run fast. It is one of the fastest running insects. Some cockroaches have wings and can fly.

A cockroach will eat anything—food, grease, trash, books, chairs, other insects. It can be found anywhereóhomes, stores, and bakeries. A cockroach is dirty and tarnishes anything it touches.

The best way to keep a cockroach out of your house is to keep your house clean and dry. A cockroach likes a house that is dirty, greasy, and damp. Seal cracks to prevent the cockroach from entering the house. Dust cracks with roach powder. The roach powder has poison in it. The poison gets on the cockroach's legs, feelers, and casing. The cockroach eats the poison as it grooms itself and soon it expires.

222 words

(continued on next page)

Clouds

Clouds are masses of condensed water vapor that float in the sky. There are many kinds of clouds. Some clouds are white and fluffy on a bright sunny sky. Some clouds are black and gray clouds that form in the darkening sky and predict rain.

In 1803, a man named Luke Howard devised a way of naming and sorting clouds. *Cirrus* clouds are curly white clouds made of drops of ice. They form high over other clouds, as much as 10 miles up in the sky. Stratus clouds form just hundreds of feet over the earth. They are thin foglike clouds that are seen early in the morning or late in the night. Cumulus clouds are the fluffy white clouds that float across the sky on a bright summer day. They move about a mile over the earth and cast shade on the ground. These clouds can have many shapes. They may look like an animal or a person or an object. After the sun sets, they dissolve into stratus clouds. Nimbus clouds are the dark rain clouds. They are brimming with water that runs into rain. Look at the sky. Can you name the clouds you see?

198 words

(continued on next page)

From Neuhaus Education Center. (1998). *Basic language skills: Concept manual, book two* (p. 66). Bellaire, TX: Author; adapted by permission. Copyright © 1998 by Neuhaus Education Center. All rights reserved. In *Multisensory Teaching of Basic Language Skills Activity Book, Revised Edition* by Suzanne Carreker and Judith R. Birsh (2011, Paul H. Brookes Publishing Co., Inc.)

The Donkey and the Thorn Bush

Once there was a farmer who was gathering baskets of juicy tomatoes, crisp green beans, and sweet corn from his garden. One by one, the farmer loaded his donkey with the baskets that were brimming with food.

"I have worked hard for all of this bounteous food. I planted the seeds and watered the young plants without fail. I tirelessly picked the weeds so that they would not choke the plants. And now I toil in the hot sun to bring this food home to my family."

The farmer continued to work as there was much food to gather. While he worked, the farmer munched on handfuls of his crisp green beans. "I am indeed a fortunate man, for there can be no better food than what I am now gathering."

The donkey stood by as the farmer labored on. As the donkey stood watching the farmer munch on his crisp green beans, he realized that he was hungry. Amid the farmer's bounteous harvest, the donkey noticed a thorn bush growing and began to eat it. "How many people would be happy with the delicacies that I am carrying on my back? But for my tastes, the sumptuous, simple thorn bush is a veritable feast," he said.

When the farmer had filled all the baskets and had loaded them on the donkey, he and the donkey returned home. Each was no longer hungry and each was satisfied with his choice.

240 words

(continued on next page)

From Carreker, S. (2004). *Developing metacognitive skill: Vocabulary and comprehension* (p. 23). Bellaire, TX: Neuhaus Education Center; adapted by permission. Copyright © 2004 by Neuhaus Education Center. All rights reserved. In *Multisensory Teaching of Basic Language Skills Activity Book, Revised Edition* by Suzanne Carreker and Judith R. Birsh (2011, Paul H. Brookes Publishing Co., Inc.)

Androcles and the Lion

Androcles was a slave who was cruelly treated. One day he had a chance to escape. He quickly ran into the forest and there he saw a lion. He was about to run when he noticed that the lion was crying heartbreakingly.

Androcles moved slowly toward the lion. The lion's paw was swollen and bleeding because a sharp thorn had gouged it. Androcles gently washed and bandaged the lion's paw.

The lion was so grateful that he licked Androcles' face just as a dog would lick its master's face. The lion then led Androcles to a cave, where he lived safely for many weeks. Each day the lion would bring Androcles fresh meat. Both Androcles and the lion were quite satisfied.

One day Androcles and the lion were both captured and taken to the arena. Androcles was to be thrown to the lion after it had been starved for several days. On the day of the grand event, the emperor and all his subjects came to view the spectacle. The lion was released from its cage.

The lion came out of the cage, roaring loudly. The lion charged toward Androcles as the crowd cheered wildly. When the lion came near Androcles, it leaped up so its front paws rested upon Androcles' shoulders. The lion then lovingly licked Androcles' face. Androcles was happy to see his friend.

The emperor had never seen such a sight before and was so moved that he freed Androcles and the lion.

246 words

(continued on next page)

From Carreker, S. (2004). *Developing metacognitive skill: Vocabulary and comprehension* (p. 11). Bellaire, TX: Neuhaus Education Center; adapted by permission. Copyright © 2004 by Neuhaus Education Center. All rights reserved. In *Multisensory Teaching of Basic Language Skills Activity Book, Revised Edition* by Suzanne Carreker and Judith R. Birsh (2011, Paul H. Brookes Publishing Co., Inc.)

The Vain Crow

Once there was a quite ordinary crow that found some brightly colored feathers that a peacock had discarded. "I shall wear these feathers and be the finest crow there is," he said to himself.

The crow found an old piece of string and painstakingly wove the brightly colored feathers to his quite ordinary tail feathers. "I am certainly the grandest crow there ever was," he said proudly as he prepared to strut about with his new look.

He first found a flock of crows and he proudly strutted before his peers, who felt ignored, despised, and distressed.

The crow then gained access to a flock of peacocks. When the peacocks detected his audaciousness, they began to peck at his pretentious feathers with their beaks. Soon the crow was disheveled and a bit wiser.

The crow humbly returned to his own kind, but they were still smarting from the crow's former rejection. They turned their backs on him.

157 words

(continued on next page)

Elephants

Elephants are the largest of all land animals and can weigh more than 12,000 pounds! The average height at the shoulder is 10 feet. At birth, an elephant calf is 3 feet tall and weighs about 200 pounds.

The two kinds of elephants are African elephants and Asian elephants. African elephants are generally heavier and taller than Asian elephants. African elephants have much larger ears, which are shaped somewhat like the continent of Africa and weigh about 110 pounds each.

Elephants feed mainly on roots, leaves, fruit, grasses, and, sometimes, tree bark. An adult elephant eats as much as 300 pounds of food a day, but it only digests half of the food it eats. Elephants sometimes walk hundreds of miles in search of water and food.

The elephant's trunk is very versatile. The elephant inhales and exhales through two nostrils at the end of its trunk. The elephant trumpets with its trunk. It can swim long distances using the trunk as a snorkel. There are fingerlike parts at the tip of the trunk, enabling the elephant to grasp objects as small as a single blade of grass. An elephant calf sucks its trunk just as a human baby sucks its thumb.

203 words

(continued on next page)

The Clydesdale

One of the most recognizable breeds of horses is the Clydesdale. If you are not familiar with the Clydesdale, watch the commercials during the next Super Bowl, and you will receive a delightful introduction. The name Clydesdale is derived from the district in Scotland where the horse was first bred. The breed was developed to meet the agricultural needs of farmers and the hauling needs of miners. The breed quickly spread throughout Scotland and northern England. Since the late 19th century, this draft or working horse has been exported all over the world.

The Clydesdale is a large breed of horse that ranges in height from 16 to 19 hands. A hand is the basic unit for measuring horses and equals 4 inches. The Clydesdale weighs between 1,600 and 2,200 pounds. The most common color is bay or reddish brown, but the horse can be black, brown, or chestnut, with roans or white hairs throughout the coat. The Clydesdale's distinctive markings include four feathery socks of long silky hair that flow from just below the knee to the hock, the part of the horse that corresponds to the human ankle. White is the preferred color for the socks, but the socks can also be black or brown.

At a horse show, a Clydesdale judge looks for a sturdy, muscular horse with an open forehead, a wide muzzle, large nostrils, bright eyes, big ears, and a well-arched neck. The judge checks to see that the horse lifts its feet easily and completely off the ground when it steps. Intelligence and an agreeable disposition add to the merits of the horse. Ultimately, the judge awards the blue ribbon to the Clydesdale that creates the best impression of strength, agility, and docility.

290 words

Fraction Lotto

1 whole							
1/2				1/2			
1/4		1/4		1/4		1/4	
1/8	1/8	1/8	1/8	1/8	1/8	1/8	1/8

Building Block Checklist for Effective Classroom Management

Directions:

1. Read through all items in the Building Block Checklist.
2. In the left column, place a check mark next to each item currently being addressed.
3. In the right column, place a check mark next to each item that needs to change to improve classroom management.

Things I am doing	Aspect of planning	Things I want to do differently
	Classroom environment	
	Bulletin boards	
	Furniture	
	Student desks	
	Traffic pattern(s)	
	Teacher organization	
	Teacher(s) desk(s)	
	Organization of teaching materials	
	Plan for instructional transitions	
	Student behavior	
	Establishment of classroom rules and expectations	
	Reduction of student anxiety	
	Bonding and connecting with all students	
	Connecting with individual students	
	Active listening to students	

(continued on next page)

From Schedler, J.-F., & Bitler, E.-F. (2004). *A classroom management secret: Keep the glasses full.* Workshop presented at the annual conference of the New York Branch of The International Dyslexia Association, New York; adapted by permission. In *Multisensory Teaching of Basic Language Skills Activity Book, Revised Edition,* by Suzanne Carreker and Judith R. Birsh (2011, Paul H. Brookes Publishing Co., Inc.)

	Self-evaluation of classroom needs	
	Is it a safe environment?	
	Can students take academic risks?	
	Are students exploring friendships?	
	Are students negotiating the classroom setting?	
	Are students learning appropriate expectations and behaviors?	
	Are students' behaviors transferable to the outside world?	

From Schedler, J.-F., & Bitler, E.-F. (2004). *A classroom management secret: Keep the glasses full.* Workshop presented at the annual conference of the New York Branch of The International Dyslexia Association, New York; adapted by permission. In *Multisensory Teaching of Basic Language Skills Activity Book, Revised Edition,* by Suzanne Carreker and Judith R. Birsh (2011, Paul H. Brookes Publishing Co., Inc.)

Answer Key

ACTIVITY 1—TERMS FOR RESEARCH AND MULTISENSORY TEACHING

1) q, 2) p, 3) k, 4) m, 5) l, 6) a, 7) d, 8) g, 9) n, 10) h, 11) e, 12) b, 13) i, 14) f, 15) c, 16) j, 17) o

ACTIVITY 2—THE BRAIN

(Labeled brain)

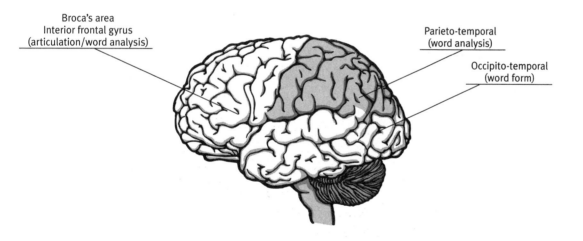

Figure 1.

ACTIVITY 3—TERMS FOR ORAL LANGUAGE

1) f, 2) e, 3) b, 4) g, 5) h, 6) a, 7) j, 8) i, 9) c, 10) d

ACTIVITY 4—PHONEMES: VOWELS

ACTIVITY 5—CLUES FOR IDENTIFYING WORD ORIGIN

1) The consonant pairs *gn, kn,* and *wr* (Anglo-Saxon); 2) roots that end in *ct* and *pt* (Latin); 3) vowel pairs (Anglo-Saxon); 4) initial consonant clusters *rh, pt, pn,* and *ps* (Greek); 5) chameleon prefixes (Latin); 6) common, everyday words (Anglo-Saxon); 7) the consonant cluster *ch* pronounced /k/ (Greek); 8) the letters *c, s,* and *t* pronounced /sh/ (Latin); 9) medial *y* (Greek); 10) consonant digraphs *ch, sh, th, wh* (Anglo-Saxon); 11) the affixing of roots (Latin); 12) compound words (Anglo-Saxon); 13) combining forms (Greek); 14) the affixing of base words (Anglo-Saxon); 15) the consonant cluster *ph* pronounced /f/ (Greek); 16) the schwa or unstressed vowel sound (Latin)

ACTIVITY 6—IDENTIFYING WORD ORIGIN

scholar (Greek), *dislike* (Anglo-Saxon), *that* (Anglo-Saxon), *construction* (Latin), *phonograph* (Greek), *made* (Anglo-Saxon), *excellent* (Latin), *boat* (Anglo-Saxon), *conductor* (Latin), *barn* (Anglo-Saxon), *microscope* (Greek), *direction* (Latin), *transport* (Latin), *symphony* (Greek), *chloroplast* (Greek), *hardware* (Anglo-Saxon), *photograph* (Greek), *shipyard* (Anglo-Saxon), *respect* (Latin), *spatial* (Latin), *water* (Anglo-Saxon), *manuscript* (Latin), *timely* (Anglo-Saxon), *portable* (Latin), *heart* (Anglo-Saxon), *good* (Anglo-Saxon), *introduction* (Latin), *transcript* (Latin), *bread* (Anglo-Saxon), *bad* (Anglo-Saxon)

ACTIVITY 7—IDENTIFYING WORD ORIGIN

food (Anglo-Saxon), *rhythm* (Greek), *lotion* (Latin), *reject* (Latin), *eruption* (Latin), *chorus* (Greek), *thermometer* (Greek), *gather* (Anglo-Saxon), *induction* (Latin), *intersect* (Latin), *psychology* (Greek), *rhododendron* (Greek), *helpless* (Anglo-Saxon), *napkin* (Anglo-Saxon), *wait* (Anglo-Saxon), *destruction* (Latin), *sympathy* (Greek), *football* (Anglo-Saxon), *illegal* (Latin), *conduct* (Latin)

ACTIVITY 8—CONSONANT PHONEMES: PLACE OF ARTICULATION

Both lips: /b/, /m/, /n/, /p/

Teeth and lower lip: /f/, /v/

Between the teeth: /th/, /th/

Ridge behind the teeth: /d/, /l/, /n/, /r/, /s/, /t/, /z/

Roof of the mouth: /ch/, /j/, /sh/, /y/, /zh/

Back of the mouth: /g/, /k/, /ng/, /w/

From the throat: /h/

ACTIVITY 9—CONSONANT PHONEMES: BLOCKED, PARTIALLY BLOCKED, AND UNBLOCKED

Blocked: /f/, /l/, /m/, /n/, /ng/, /r/, /s/, /sh/, /th/, /th/, /v/, /w/, /z/, /zh/

Partially blocked: /b/, /ch/, /d/, /g/, /j/, /k/, /p/, /t/, /y/

Unblocked: /h/

ACTIVITY 10—PHONEMES: VOICED AND UNVOICED CONSONANTS

Voiced: /b/, /d/, /g/, /j/, /l/, /m/, /n/, /ng/, /r/, /th/, /v/, /w/, /y/, /z/, /zh/

Unvoiced: /ch/, /f/, /h/, /hw/, /k/, /p/, /s/, /sh/, /t/, /th/

ACTIVITY 11—CONSONANT PHONEMES: COGNATES

Cognates: /ch/ and /j/, /t/ and /d/, /f/ and /v/, /k/ and /g/, /p/ and /b/, /s/ and /z/, /sh/ and /zh, /th/ and /th/

ACTIVITY 12—CONSONANT PHONEMES: CONTINUANT AND CLIPPED

/t/ (clipped), /m/ (continuant), /p/ (clipped), /n/ (continuant), /s/ (continuant), /l/ (continuant), /j/ (clipped), /b/ (clipped), /g/ (clipped), /v/ (continuant), /y/ (clipped), /r/ (continuant), /z/ (continuant), /d/ (clipped)

ACTIVITY 13—PHONEME CHECKLIST

/l/ as in *leaf* (voiced, continuant, blocked)

/d/ as in *dog* (voiced, partially blocked, clipped)

/g/ as in *goat* (voiced, partially blocked, clipped)

/b/ as in *bat* (voiced, partially blocked, clipped)

/th/ as in *thin* (continuant, unvoiced, blocked)

/ch/ as in *chin* (partially blocked, unvoiced, clipped)

/w/ as in *wagon* (voiced, continuant, blocked)

/h/ as in *house* (open, unvoiced)

/h/ is the only consonant sound that opens the mouth; all other consonant sounds are blocked or partially blocked.

/m/ as in *mitten* (voiced, continuant, blocked)

/j/ as in *jump* (voiced, partially blocked, clipped)

/zh/ as in *erosion* (voiced, continuant, blocked)

/s/ as in *sock* (continuant, unvoiced, blocked)

ACTIVITY 14—PHONEME CHECKLIST

/y/ as in *yellow* (voiced, partially blocked, clipped)

/z/ as in *zipper* (voiced, continuant, blocked)

/n/ as in *nest* (voiced, continuant, blocked)

/ng/ as in *sink* (voiced, continuant, blocked)

/k/ as in *kite* (partially blocked, unvoiced, clipped)

/p/ as in *pig* (partially blocked, unvoiced, clipped)

/sh/ as in *ship* (continuant, unvoiced, blocked)

/t/ as in *table* (partially blocked, unvoiced, clipped)

/f/ as in *fish* (continuant, unvoiced, blocked)

/th/ as in *mother* (voiced, continuant, blocked)

/v/ as in *valentine* (voiced, continuant, blocked)

/r/ as in *rabbit* (voiced, continuant, blocked)

ACTIVITY 15—CLASSIFICATION OF PHONEMES

1) b, 2) e, 3) c, 4) a, 5) f, 6) d, 7) i, 8) g, 9) j, 10) h, 11) l, 12) k

ACTIVITY 16—PHONEMIC AWARENESS ACTIVITIES

Isolation/identification: 4, 6, 8, 11

Blending: 1, 12

Segmentation: 3, 7, 10

Deletion/addition: 2, 5, 9

ACTIVITY 17—HOW MANY PHONEMES?

mat (3), *cash* (3), *ship* (3), *match* (3), *stop* (4), *knife* (3), *scratch* (5), *truck,* (4), *love* (3), *spell* (4), *stand* (5), *child* (4), *month* (4), *think* (4), *peach* (3), *queen* (4), *train* (4), *climb* (4), *strike* (5), *blank* (5)

ACTIVITY 18—HOW MANY PHONEMES?

show (2), splint (6), knee (2), badge (3), past (4), face (3), thrill (4), clock (4), give (3), shack (3), strand (6), teeth (3), church (3), shrink (5), enough (4), quit (4), fix (4), smile (4), night (3), flax (5)

ACTIVITY 19—SAME PHONEME?

(yes = the phonemes are the same; no = the phonemes are different)

*s*ai*d*/*b*e*d* (yes); *spins/spins* (no); *bath/safe* (no); *st*ea*k/*v*ein* (yes); *night/tie* (yes); *m*arket/*m*ustard (no); *that/*v*ase* (no); *peach/priest* (yes); *plaid/blast* (yes); *orbit/actor* (no); *arch/echo* (no); *splint/jumped* (yes); *sink/sing* (yes); *first/fern* (yes); *tense/face* (yes); *fly/penny* (no); *rhythm/rhyme* (no); *zipper/pansy* (yes); *graft/graph* (yes); *landed/seemed (no)*

ACTIVITY 20—SAME PHONEME?

(yes = the phonemes are the same; no = the phonemes are different)

v*iew/shoe* (yes); wash/mash (no); tent/tent (no); boy/boil (yes); canyon/yellow (yes); doctor/shortage (no); shack/wash (yes); isle/spy (yes); room/fruit (yes); ballet/survey (yes); that/with (no); single/finger (yes); jeep/girl (no); raw/haul (yes); gem/jet (yes); water/polish (yes); heal/health (no); group/grout (no); troop/soup (yes); gas/his (no)

ACTIVITY 21—HOW MANY LETTERS AND HOW MANY PHONEMES?

broom (5, 4); knee (4, 2); shrimp (6, 5); splint (6, 6); sprint (6, 6); lead (4, 3); grasp (5, 5); sound (5, 4); blame (5, 4); sing (4, 3); mix (3, 4); show (4, 2); left (4, 4); child (5, 4); space (5, 4); teach (5, 3); both (4, 3); spend (5, 5); kind (4, 4); knowledge (9, 5)

ACTIVITY 22—HOW MANY LETTERS AND HOW MANY PHONEMES?

judge (5, 3); need (4, 3); peach (5, 3); thrill (6, 4); know (4, 2); plan (4, 4); clasp (5, 5); knife (5, 3); may (3, 2); stray (5, 4); most (4, 4); shout (5, 3); shrill (6, 4); less (4, 3); close (5, 4); cloth (5, 4); splice (6, 5); trend (5, 5); jacket (6, 5); muskrat (7, 7)

ACTIVITY 23—LETTER SHAPES AND NAMES

All straight lines	All curved lines	Straight and curved lines
A, E, F, H, I K, L, M, N, T, V, W, X, Y, Z, i, k, l, t, v, w, x, y, z	C, O, S, U, c, o, s	B, D, G, J, P, Q, R, a, b, d, e, f, g, h, j, m, n, p, q, r, u

ACTIVITY 24—QUARTILES FOR DICTIONARY WORK

First quartile   A, B, C, D

Second quartile   E, F, G, H, I, J, K, L

Third quartile   M, N, O, P, Q, R

Fourth quartile   S, T, U, V, W, X, Y, Z

L (second), C (first), X (fourth), O (third), B (first), S (fourth), J (second), L (second), I (second), Q (third) graph (second), review (third), which (fourth), develop (first), kangaroo (second), never (third), compare (first), model (third), theme (fourth), pumpkin (third)

ACTIVITY 25—GUIDE WORDS FOR DICTIONARY WORK

jump (before the page); *justice* (on the page, second column); *juxtaposition* (after the page); *judicial* (before the page): *jungle* (on the page, first column); *junket* (on the page, first column); *July* (before the page); *juxtapose* (after the page); *juice* (before the page); *jury* (on the page, second column)

ACTIVITY 26—TERMS FOR PHONOLOGICAL AWARENESS AND ALPHABET KNOWLEDGE

1) d, 2) c, 3) g, 4) f, 5) b, 6) a, 7) h, 8) e, 9) o, 10) l, 11) j, 12) m, 13) i, 14) n, 15) k

ACTIVITY 27—PLANNING LESSONS FOR PHONOLOGICAL AWARENESS, ALPHABET KNOWLEDGE, AND HISTORY OF LANGUAGE

Lesson plans will vary.

ACTIVITY 28—CONTINUOUS MANUSCRIPT HANDWRITING

1) c, 2) f, 3) l, 4) e, 5) h, 6) k, 7) a, 8) g, 9) j, 10) i, 11) d, 12) b

ACTIVITY 29—APPROACH STROKES FOR CURSIVE LETTERS

Swing up, stop: i, j, p, r, s, t, u, w

Push up and over: m, n, v, x, y, z

Curve under, over, stop: a, c, d, g, o, q

Curve way up, loop left: b, e, f, h, k, l

ACTIVITY 30—CURSIVE HANDWRITING STROKE DESCRIPTIONS

1) i, 2) c, 3) d, 4) a, 5) f, 6) h, 7) j, 8) k, 9) g, 10) e, 11) l, 12) b

ACTIVITY 31—HANDWRITING PRACTICE

Introduction and Practice Activities
1. Students sky write a new letter as the teacher describes the letter strokes.
2. Students trace a model of the new letter several times with their fingers.
3. Students trace a model of a new letter with a pencil.
4. Students copy a model of new letter on paper.
5. Students write a new letter from memory.
Practice Activities
6. Students trace a model of a series of letters that share the same approach stroke.
7. Students write a dictated series of letters that share the same approach stroke.
8. Students trace a model of a series of letters that contain different approach strokes.
9. Students write a dictated series of letters that contain different approach strokes.
10. Students copy words from the board.
11. Students write letters with attention to proportion.

ACTIVITY 32—PLANNING LESSONS FOR HANDWRITING

Lesson plans will vary.

ACTIVITY 33—SOUND–SYMBOL CORRESPONDENCES

One frequent sound: *b, d, f, h, j, k, l, m, p, q, r, t, v, w, z*

More than one frequent sound: *a, e, i, o, u, c, g, n, s, x, y*

ACTIVITY 34—PRACTICE WORDS

Answers will vary. Sample words include the following: *at, fat, hat, pat, sat, had, lad, pad, sad, lap, nap, sap, tap, fan, pan, tan, lag, sag, tag, bit, fit, hit, lit, pit, sit, in, fin, pin, sin, tin, dip, hip, lip, nip, sip, tip, did, hid, lid, hop, mop, pop, top, dot, got, lot, dog, fog, hog, log, nod, flat, glad, slap, snap, and, hand, land, sand, ant, pant, slant, flag, snag, stag, fast, last, past, flit, spit, slip, snip, fist, list, hint, silk, stop, slot*

ACTIVITY 35—MAKING DIALOGUES TO MAKE WORDS

Dialogues will vary.

ACTIVITY 36—PLANNING LESSONS FOR BEGINNING READING

Lesson plans will vary.

ACTIVITY 37—READING PATTERNS

c is pronounced /k/ before *a, o, u*, or any consonant.

c is pronounced /s/ before *e, i*, or *y*.

g is pronounced /g/ before *a, o, u*, or any consonant.

g is pronounced /j/ before *e, i*, or *y*.

n is pronounced /n/ in initial, final, or medial position.

n is pronounced /ng/ before any letter that is pronounced /k/ or /g/.

x is pronounced /ks/ in medial or final position.

x is pronounced /z/ in initial position.

y is pronounced /y/ in initial position.

y is pronounced /ī/ at the end of an accented syllable.

y is pronounced /ē/ at the end of a word in an unaccented syllable.

ACTIVITY 38—HARD AND SOFT *c* AND *g*

<u>c</u>ity (soft before *i*), <u>g</u>em (soft before *e*), <u>c</u>lown (hard before a consonant), <u>c</u>ent (soft before *e*), fan<u>c</u>y (soft before *y*), <u>g</u>ym (soft before *y*), <u>g</u>ist (soft before *i*), spa<u>c</u>e (soft before *e*), ener<u>g</u>y (soft before *y*), in<u>c</u>lusion (hard before a consonant), exi<u>g</u>ent (soft before *e*), fa<u>c</u>ility (soft before *i*), <u>g</u>entleman (soft before *e*), bi<u>c</u>ycle (soft before *y*), bi<u>c</u>ycle (hard before a consonant), diffi<u>c</u>ult (hard before *u*), re<u>g</u>istration (soft before *i*), fa<u>c</u>ulty (hard before *u*), spa<u>c</u>e (soft before *e*), <u>g</u>eneral (soft before *e*), <u>c</u>eiling (soft before *e*)

ACTIVITY 39—LETTER CLUSTERS

bl (blend), *sh* (digraph), *mp* (blend), *th* (digraph), *nk* (blend), *nt* (blend), *ck* (digraph), *wh* (digraph), *ch* (digraph), *dr* (blend)

The vowel pairs *ea, oe, oo, oa, ai, au, aw* are digraphs; *oi, ou,* and *oy* are diphthongs. (*Note:* The vowel pair *ou* as in *soup* is considered a digraph; however, it is infrequently used.)

ACTIVITY 40—HOW MANY LETTERS AND HOW MANY GRAPHEMES?

bridge (6, 4); *wheel* (5, 3); *church* (6, 3); *school* (6, 4); *show* (4, 2); *band* (4, 4); *feet* (4, 3); *knife* (5, 3); *phone* (5, 3); *song* (4, 3); *breath* (6, 4); *slant* (5, 5); *stack* (5, 4); *shack* (5, 3); *sketch* (6, 4); *hand* (4, 4); *finish* (6, 5); *straw* (5, 4); *head* (4, 3); *shroud* (6, 4)

ACTIVITY 41—HOW MANY LETTERS AND HOW MANY GRAPHEMES?

deck (4, 3); *lamp* (4, 4); *bench* (5, 4); *smoke* (5, 4); *glow* (4, 3); *shrine* (6, 4); *cheese* (6, 3); *pencil* (6, 6); *state* (5, 4); *strong* (6, 5); *teacher* (7, 4); *phone* (5, 3); *sports* (6, 5); *plate* (5, 4); *stretch* (7, 5); *strand* (6, 6); *clover* (6, 5); *start* (5, 4); *seed* (4, 3); *threat* (6, 4)

ACTIVITY 42—VOWEL PAIRS

The first vowel does the talking: *ai* (paint), *ay* (play), *ea* (teach), *ee* (feet), *ei* (ceiling), *ey* (monkey), *ie* (tie), *oa* (boat), *oe* (toe), *ow* (show), *ue* (statue)

The first vowel does not do the talking: *au* (saucer), *aw* (saw), *ea* (head), *ea* (steak), *ei* (vein), *eu* (Europe), *ew* (pew), *ie* (priest), *oi* (oil), *oo* (book), *oo* (moon), *ou* (out), *ow* (cow), *oy* (boy), *ui* (fruit)

ACTIVITY 43—VOWEL-*r* PATTERNS

/er/: *ar* (dollar), *er* (fern), *er* (letter), *ir* (first), *ir* (tapir), *or* (doctor), *or* (work), *ur* (fur), *ur* (murmur)

/ar/: *ar* (star)

/or/: *ar* (warm), *ar* (quart), *or* (fork)

The combinations *er, ir,* and *ur* are always pronounced /er/.

In an accented syllable, *ar* is pronounced /ar/ and *or* is pronounced /or/.

In an unaccented syllable, *ar* and *or* are pronounced /er/.

After /w/, *or* is pronounced /er/.

After /w/, *ar* is pronounced /or/.

ACTIVITY 44—SYLLABLE TYPE DEFINITIONS

1) d, 2) e, 3) f, 4) c, 5) a, 6) b

ACTIVITY 45—SORTING SYLLABLE TYPES: CLOSED, OPEN, VOWEL-*r*

Open: *so, he, me, we*

Closed: *hiss, sod, hen, hem, met, west, fond, hand, spun, cat, fist*

Vowel-*r*: *firm, car, spur, fork, hard*

ACTIVITY 46—SORTING SYLLABLE TYPES: CLOSED, OPEN, VOWEL PAIRS

Open: *so, fly, be, cry, me*

Closed: *miss, help, bond, stomp, send*

Vowel pairs: *seed, toast, book, heap, maid, free, deep, moo, bee, play*

ACTIVITY 47—SORTING SYLLABLE TYPES

Closed: *not, hen, mettle, men, hit, lost, shamble, pick, picture, went*

Open: *no, noble, he, me, hi, locate, she, supreme, so, we, my*

Vowel-consonant-*e*: *note, here, hive, lone, lore, shine, supreme, mine, locate*

Vowel-*r*: *nor, her, short, portion, work, warm, marble*

Vowel pair: *noon, heat, meet, mean, loan, low, sheep, pie, peek, soak, weep*

Final stable or consonant-*le*: *noble, mettle, picture, portion, marble, shamble*

ACTIVITY 48—WHICH SYLLABLE TYPE?

lump (closed), *smoke* (vowel-consonant-*e*), *she* (open), *speech* (vowel pair), *clutch* (closed), *strict* (closed), *thirst* (vowel-*r*), *porch* (vowel-*r*), *stray* (vowel pair), *bottle* (final stable or consonant-*le*), *monster* (vowel-*r*), *moisture* (vowel pair), *simple* (final stable or consonant-*le*), *hundred* (closed), *solo* (vowel-consonant-*e*), *perfect* (vowel-*r*), *extreme* (vowel-consonant-*e*), *publish* (closed), *circle* (consonant-*le*), *frequent* (open)

ACTIVITY 49—GENERATING SYLLABLE TYPES

Answers will vary.

ACTIVITY 50—SYLLABLE DIVISION PATTERNS

mascot (VCCV), rotate (VCV), monster (VCCCV), bias (VV), tactic (VCCV), cabin (VCV), lion (VV), supreme (VCCV), portray (VCCCV), second (VCV), pumpkin (VCCCV), truant (VV), surround (VCCV), instant (VCCCV), item (VCV), convoy (VCCV), instinct (VCCCV), report (VCV), contrast (VCCCV), connect (VCCV)

ACTIVITY 51—WHERE TO DIVIDE WORDS: VCCV OR VCV?

chip munk, lo tus, dis tance, pig ment, en tice, ban ner, du ty, de tain, es cape, ba by, par ty, pro vide, lo cal, stub born, be low, mar ket, lo cate, cop per, re late, rib bon

ACTIVITY 52—WHERE TO DIVIDE WORDS: VCCCV OR VCV?

cha os, li on, dis trict, po em, ex treme, con struct, du et, des troy, pump kin, musk rat, part ner, ru in, du al, dis tract, bi as, con tract, da is, tru ant, mis spell, spec trum

ACTIVITY 53—ACCENT

spi' der, **bo'** a, pre **dict'**, **con'** stant, con **trol'**, **na'** vy, **qui'** et, pas **tel'**, **en'** ter, can **teen'** , **sev'** en, be **cause'**, **cham'** ber, **con'** voy, **tri'** al, **spec'** trum, **pump'** kin, **tri'** umph, de **cide'**, **chal'** lenge

ACTIVITY 54—SYLLABLE DIVISION PATTERNS AND CHOICES

mascot (VCCV, first); rotate (VCV, first); monster (VCCCV, first); bias (VV, first); tactic (VCCV, first); cabin (VCV, third); lion (VV, first); supreme (VCCV, second); portray (VCCCV, second); second (VCV, third); pumpkin (VCCCV, third); truant (VV, second); surround (VCCV, second); instant (VCCCV, first); item (VCV, first); convoy (VCCV, first); instinct (VCCCV, second); report (VCV, second); contrast (VCCCV, first and second); connect (VCCV, second)

ACTIVITY 55—SHORT VOWELS IN VOWEL-*r* SYLLABLES

m<u>er</u>ry (/ĕ/), c<u>or</u>ner (/or/ /er/), f<u>ir</u>st (/er/), c<u>ar</u>ry (/ă/), v<u>er</u>y (/ĕ/), s<u>ur</u>vey (/er/), ch<u>er</u>ry (/ĕ/), <u>er</u>rand (/ĕ/), g<u>ar</u>lic (/ar/), d<u>er</u>rick (/ĕ/), f<u>er</u>ret (/ĕ/), sh<u>er</u>bet (/er/), m<u>er</u>it (/ĕ/), b<u>ar</u>rack (/ă/), h<u>ar</u>ness (/ar/), <u>er</u>ror (/ĕ/), <u>or</u>bit (/or/), c<u>ar</u>rot (/ă/), <u>ur</u>gent (/er/), n<u>ar</u>row (/ă/)

ACTIVITY 56—TERMS FOR DECODING

1) j, 2) b, 3) e, 4) i, 5) k, 6) d, 7) m, 8) f, 9) n, 10) h, 11) a, 12) p, 13) g, 14) o, 15) c, 16) l

ACTIVITY 57—VOWEL AND CONSONANT SUFFIXES

Vowel suffixes: *-en, -ity, -ous, -able, -ish, -ist*

Consonant suffixes: *-ment, -ful, -ness, -less, -ly, -ward*

ACTIVITY 58—INFLECTIONAL ENDING -*s*

seems /z/, jumps /s/, lands /z/, starts /s/, lists /s/, picks /s/, likes /s/, settles /z/, copes /s/, spells /z/, camps /s/, distributes /s/, recycles /z/, screams /z/, grasps /s/

ACTIVITY 59—INFLECTIONAL ENDING *-ed*

seemed (/d/), jumped (/t/), landed (/ed/), started (/ed/), tossed (/t/), picked (/t/), listed (/ed/), settled (/d/), copied (/d/), spelled (/d/), camped (/t/), distributed (/ed/), recycled (/d/), enclosed (/d/), realized (/d/)

ACTIVITY 60—INFLECTIONAL AND DERIVATIONAL SUFFIXES

Base word	Part of speech	Derivative	Part of speech	Ending or suffix	Inflectional	Derivational
desk	noun	desks	noun	-s	✓	
help	verb	helpless	adjective	-less		✓
big	adjective	bigger	adjective	-er	✓	
mow	noun or verb	mowing	noun or verb	-ing	✓	
play	noun or verb	playful	adjective	-ful		✓
sky	noun	skies	noun	-s	✓	
bleed	verb	bleeding	noun or verb	-ing	✓	
copy	noun or verb	copying	noun or verb	-ing	✓	
dark	adjective	darkness	noun	-ness		✓
keep	verb	keeper	noun	-er		✓
merry	adjective	merriment	noun	-ment	✓	

ACTIVITY 61—IRREGULAR WORDS FOR READING

shoe, country, busy, ghost, lamb, said, does, doubt, four, ocean, enough, aisle, friend, plaid, from, would, two, colonel

ACTIVITY 62—REGULAR OR IRREGULAR FOR READING?

done (I), down (R), one (I), tone (R), again (I), paint (R), seed (R), seat (R), came (R), come (I), lose (I), lone (R), back (R), buy (I), pretty (I), plenty (R), become (I), began (R), any (I), orange (I)

ACTIVITY 63—REGULAR OR IRREGULAR FOR READING?

couch (R), some (I), whose (I), could (I), sole (R), soul (I), eye (I), many (I), trust (R), truth (I), debt (I), dead (R), people (I), queen (R), between (R), together (I), trouble (I), tremble (R), woman (I), were (I), should (I), where (I), why (R), match (R)

ACTIVITY 64—THE ART AND SCIENCE OF FLUENCY INSTRUCTION

Answers will vary.

ACTIVITY 65—MEASURING PROSODY

Rubrics will vary.

ACTIVITY 66—TERMS FOR DECODING AND FLUENCY

1) g, 2) o, 3) h, 4) d, 5) a, 6) i, 7) n, 8) l, 9) m, 10) b, 11) f, 12) j, 13) c, 14) e, 15) k, 16) p

ACTIVITY 67—SPELLING PATTERNS

1) e, 2) f, 3) c, 4) a, 5) b, 6) d, 7) j, 8) g, 9) i, 10) l, 11) h, 12) k, 13) m, 14) q, 15) p, 16) r, 17) o, 18) n

ACTIVITY 68—IDENTIFYING SPELLING PATTERNS

employ, /oi/, final /oi/ is spelled *oy*

ground, /ou/, medial /ou/ is spelled *ou*

giant, /j/, /j/ before *i* is spelled *g*

green, /ē/, medial /ē/ in a one-syllable word is spelled *ee*

match, /ch/, final /ch/ after a short vowel in a one-syllable word is spelled *tch*

tuna, /ŭ/, final /ŭ/ is spelled *a*

polite, /ō/, /ō/ at the end of a syllable is spelled *o*

candy, /k/, /k/ before *a* is spelled *c*

lilac, /k/, final /k/ after a short vowel in a multisyllabic word is spelled *c*

ugly, /ē/, final /ē/ at the end of a word with two or more syllables is spelled *y*

porch, /ch/, final /ch/ after a consonant is spelled *ch*

shy, /ī/, final /ī/ is spelled *y*

wasp, /ŏ/, /ŏ/ after *w* is spelled *a*

block, /k/, final /k/ after a short vowel in a one-syllable word is spelled *ck*

dodge, /j/, final /j/ after a short vowel in a one-syllable word is spelled *dge*

skill, /k/, /k/ before *i* is spelled *k*

tray, /ā/, /ā/ in final position is spelled *ay*

flee, /ē/, final /ē/ in a one-syllable word is spelled *ee*

ACTIVITY 69—PARTIAL OR COMPLETE PHONETIC REPRESENTATION FOR SPELLING

st for *seat* (partial), *kat* for *cat* (complete), *ct* for *seat* (complete), *gv* for *give* (partial), *whl* for *while* (partial), *jumpt* for *jumped* (complete), *rede* for *read* (complete), *yl* for *while* (complete), *sop* for *soap* (complete), *plez* for *please* (complete), *sep* for *step* (partial), *pik* for *pick* (complete), *mn* for *man* (partial), *moshun* for *motion* (complete), *teme* for *team* (complete), *cunty* for *country* (partial), *hav* for *have* (complete), *samd* for *seemed* (partial), *batel* for *battle* (complete), *enuf* for *enough* (complete), *lafent* for *elephant* (complete), *selebr8* for *celebrate* (complete), *site* for *city* (complete), *split* for *splint* (partial), *sd* for *said* (partial), *wun* for *one* (complete)

ACTIVITY 70—FIVE SPELLING RULES

1) b, 2) c, 3) a, 4) e, 5) d

ACTIVITY 71—RULE WORDS

hills (hill + s; the Floss Rule)

letters (letter + s; the Rabbit Rule)

swimmer (swim + er; the Doubling Rule)

happiness (happy + ness; the Changing Rule)

racer (race + er; the Dropping Rule)

dresses (dress + es; the Floss Rule)

reddish (red + ish; the Doubling Rule)

beginning (begin + ing; the Doubling Rule)

penniless (penny + less; the Changing Rule)

muffins (muffin + s; the Rabbit Rule)

engaging (engage + ing; the Dropping Rule)

omitted (omit + ed; the Doubling Rule)

plentiful (plenty + ful; the Changing Rule)

enticing (entice + ing; the Dropping Rule)

settled (settle + ed; the Dropping Rule)

emptied (empty + ed; the Changing Rule)

preferred (prefer + ed; the Doubling Rule)

permitted (permit + ed; the Doubling Rule)

ACTIVITY 72—CHECKPOINTS FOR THE DOUBLING RULE

	One vowel	One consonant	One accent	Vowel suffix	Derivative
hot + est	✓	✓	✓	✓	hottest
run + er	✓	✓	✓	✓	runner
star + ing	✓	✓	✓	✓	starring
cup + ful	✓	✓	✓		cupful
steep + est		✓	✓	✓	steepest
stand + ing	✓		✓	✓	standing
camp + er	✓		✓	✓	camper
child + ish	✓		✓	✓	childish
art + ist	✓		✓	✓	artist
open + er	✓	✓		✓	opener
begin + er	✓	✓	✓	✓	beginner
benefit + ed	✓	✓		✓	benefited[a]
omit + ed	✓	✓	✓	✓	omitted
travel + *ing*	✓	✓	✓	✓	traveled[a]
forget + able	✓	✓	✓	✓	forgettable

[a]The preferred spelling of these words in the United States is without the doubled final consonant in the base word, which matches the Doubling Rule. In the United Kingdom, the doubled final consonant in the base word is preferred.

ACTIVITY 73—ANALYZING WORDS FOR SPELLING

Regular	**Rule**	**Irregular (the irregular part is underlined)**
pitch	batting	gl<u>o</u>ve
homerun	runner	<u>one</u>
three	slider	n<u>o</u>thing
shortstop		s<u>ea</u>son
player		
manager		
strike		
foul		

ACTIVITY 74—REGULAR, RULE, OR IRREGULAR FOR SPELLING

Regular	Rule	Irregular (the irregular part is underlined)
banana	cherry	ras<u>p</u>berry
lime	strawberry	<u>orange</u>
grape	apple	k<u>iwi</u>
coconut	pineapple	p<u>ea</u>r
sand	swimmer	o<u>ce</u>an
water	sunning	lifeg<u>u</u>ard
starfish	jellyfish	<u>sw</u>ordfish
waves	diving	se<u>a</u>weed

ACTIVITY 75—REGULAR OR IRREGULAR FOR READING AND SPELLING?

spend (regular for reading and spelling)

said (irregular for reading—The word should be pronounced /sād/—and irregular for spelling—The word should be spelled *sed*.)

have (irregular for reading—The *a* should be pronounced as a long vowel—and regular for spelling—English base words do not end in *v* so the *e* must be added.)

stroke (regular for reading and spelling)

arbor (regular for reading—Final *or* in an unaccented syllable is pronounced /er/—and irregular for spelling—The most frequent spelling of final /er/ is *er*.)

weight (regular for reading – *eigh* is pronounced /ā/; irregular for spelling—The most frequent spelling of medial a in a one-syllable word is *a*-consonant-*e*.)

soon (regular for reading and spelling)

get (irregular for reading—*g* before *i* should be pronounced /j/—and regular for spelling)

bus (irregular for reading – One final s after a short vowel in a one-syllable word is pronounced /z/— and irregular for spelling—Final *s* after a short vowel in a one-syllable word should be spelled *ss*.)

relive (irregular for reading—the *i* should be pronounced as a long vowel—and regular for spelling. English words do not end in *v* so the *e* must be added.)

ACTIVITY 76—PLANNING LESSONS FOR SPELLING

Lesson plans will vary.

ACTIVITY 77—MORPHEMES, ORIGINS, MEANINGS, AND DERIVATIVES

The example derivatives do not represent a complete list.

Morpheme	Origin	Meaning	Derivatives
ang	Latin	bend	angle, angular, triangle
astro	Greek	star	astronomy, astrology, astronaut
auto	Greek	self, unaided	autonomy, automatic, autograph
bio	Greek	life	biology, biodegradable, biography
chron	Greek	time	chronicle, chronometer, synchronize
cogn	Latin	know	recognize, cognitive, metacognition
cred	Latin	believe	creed, incredible, credulous
duct	Latin	lead	conduct, induction, deductive
fer	Latin	bear	suffer, infer, refer, confer
geo	Greek	earth	geology, geometry, geodesic
logy	Greek	study of	phonology, morphology, theology
manu	Latin	hand	manual, manuscript, manipulate
pop	Latin	people	population, populace, popular
rupt	Latin	break	interrupt, erupt, irrupt
trans	Latin	across	transport, transfer, transportation
vac	Latin	empty	vacuum, vacate, vacation
vert, vers	Latin	turn	invert, revert, reversible
vis	Latin	see	vision, visible, invisible

ACTIVITY 78—ROOTS AND COMBINING FORMS

(The example derivatives do not represent a complete list.)

ject (to throw): *reject, object, abject, project, eject, subject*

ped (foot): *pedal, pedestal, pedestrian*

spect (to watch): *inspect, respect, spectator, spectacular, speculate*

graph (to write, record): *autograph, photograph, phonograph*

bio (life): *biology, autobiography, biosphere*

ology (study of): *geology, theology, phonology*

syn, sym (same): *synchronize, synagogue, sympathy, symphony*

form (shape): *uniform, formation, transform*

cur (to go, flow): *current, curriculum, concur*

nom (to name): *nominee, nomination, nominal*

greg (to gather, group): *congregate, segregate, integrate, aggregate*

voc (to call): *vocal, vocation, vocabulary, invocation*

nym (to name): *synonym, antonym, pseudonym*

pod (foot): *tripod, podium, podiatrist*

cycl (circle): *bicycle, tricycle, cycle*

struct (to build): *construction, instruction, destruction*

vis (to see): *vision, visible, visor, supervisor*

meter (measure): *thermometer, kilometer, odometer, barometer*

ACTIVITY 79—SYLLABLES AND MORPHEMES

instructor (3, 3); autograph (3, 2); destruction (3, 3); salamander (4, 1); unleaded (3,3); waits (1, 2); interjection; (4, 3); bookkeeper (3, 3); conjunction (3, 3); photographic (4, 3); rattlesnake (3, 2); marker (2, 2); cucumber (3, 1); barbecue (3, 1); manuscript (3, 2); outstanding (3, 3); handshake (2, 2); bluebonnet (3, 2)

ACTIVITY 80—SYLLABLES AND MORPHEMES

population (4, 2); combination (4, 2); mustang (2, 1); summertime (3, 2); thermostat (3, 2); bumblebee (3, 2); protection (3, 3); wheelbarrow (3, 2); ambulance (3, 2); river (2, 1); watermelon (4, 2); canine (2, 1); dressmaker (3, 3); mercury (3, 1); countryside (3, 2); computing (3, 3); kangaroo (3, 1); vegetables (3, 2)

ACTIVITY 81—SEMANTIC WORD WEBS

Answers will vary; one possibility is shown here.

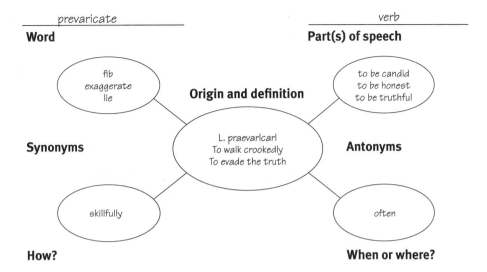

_____prevaricate_____
Word

_____verb_____
Part(s) of speech

fib
exaggerate
lie

Origin and definition

to be candid
to be honest
to be truthful

L. praevarlcarl
To walk crookedly
To evade the truth

Synonyms

Antonyms

skillfully

often

How?

When or where?

Often politicians skillfully prevaricate about their pasts.
Sentence

ACTIVITY 82—DERIVATIVE WEBS

Answers will vary; one possibility is shown here.

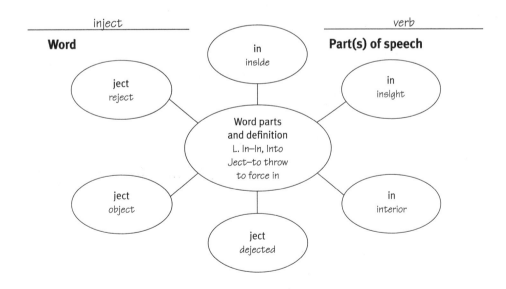

_____inject_____
Word

in
inslde

_____verb_____
Part(s) of speech

ject
reject

in
inslght

Word parts
and definition
L. In—In, Into
Ject—to throw
to force in

ject
object

in
interior

ject
dejected

The doctor will inject the vaccine through a syringe.
Sentence

ACTIVITY 83 — MULTIPLE MEANING WEBS

Answers will vary; one possibility is shown here.

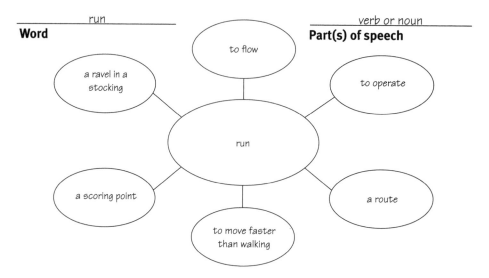

Word: <u>run</u>

Part(s) of speech: <u>verb or noun</u>

- to flow
- a ravel in a stocking
- to operate
- run
- a scoring point
- a route
- to move faster than walking

Sentence: <u>The milkman will finish his run a little after ten.</u>

ACTIVITY 84 — SEMANTIC FEATURE ANALYSIS

Answers will vary.

ACTIVITY 85 — WORD PROFILES

Word: like

Number of phonemes: 3   Phonemes: /l/, /ī/, /k/

Rime pattern: *ike* as in *bike, hike, Mike, pike, strike*

Number of letters: 4   Letters: l, i, k, e

Number of graphemes: 3   Graphemes: l, i-e, k

Spelling pattern(s): medial /ī/ in a one-syllable base word is spelled *i*-consonant-*e*

Origin: Anglo-Saxon

Derivatives: likeness, liked, likes, homelike

Answers to other parts of the word profile will vary.

ACTIVITY 86—WORD PROFILES

Word: play

Number of phonemes: 3   Phonemes: /p/, /l/, /ā/

Rime pattern: ay as in bay, day, hay, lay, may, pay, ray, say, stay, tray, slay

Number of letters: 4   Letters: p, l, a, y

Number of graphemes: 3   Graphemes: p, l, ay

Spelling pattern(s): final /ā/ is spelled ay

Origin: Anglo-Saxon

Derivatives: playful, player, plays, played

Answer to other parts of the word profile (parts of speech, multiple meanings, synonyms, antonyms, usage, and figurative uses) will vary.

ACTIVITY 87—TIERS OF VOCABULARY WORDS

Tier One	Tier Two*	Tier Three*
hunt	relate	esophagus
napkin	important	rhetoric
health	erupt	dysplasia
forest	declare	euphemism
knowledge	interpret	geriatric
happening	discontent	protoplasm
	featured	
	specific	

*Tier Two and Three words may vary according to students' experiences.

ACTIVITY 88—STUDENT-FRIENDLY DEFINITIONS

Student-friendly definitions will vary.

ACTIVITY 89—PRECISION IN USE OF VOCABULARY

Answers will vary, but the less intensive words might include *down, low, sad, glum, blue, sullen, cheerless, forlorn, gloomy, disappointed, sorrowful, somber,* and *discontented.*

The more intensive words might include *despondent, disconsolate, devastated, pessimistic, depressed, distraught,* and *dejected.*

Because of the rain, the picnic was canceled, and the children were (*sad, disappointed, glum*, etc.) but not (*distraught, depressed, despondent*, and so forth).

The hurricane completely destroyed the town, and the people were not just (*gloomy, forlorn, cheerless*, etc.); they were (*devastated, distraught, despondent*, and so forth).

Example of gradient antonyms: *satisfied, content, pleased, glad, happy, delighted, cheerful, joyful, merry, bubbly, thrilled, excited, jovial, buoyant, overjoyed, elated, ecstatic, exhilarated, euphoric, rapturous*

ACTIVITY 90—COMPREHENSION: SUMMARIZATION

Summaries will vary.

ACTIVITY 91—COMPREHENSION: SUMMARIZATION

Summaries will vary.

ACTIVITY 92—COMPREHENSION: QUESTIONING

Examples of questions for the passage *The Cockroach*:

Text explicit:

What does a cockroach eat?

Text implicit:

Why have cockroaches survived for so long?

Script implicit (or *scriptal*):

What other insect shares the same infamous reputation and why?

Examples of questions for the passage *The Clydesdale*:

Text explicit:

1. Where was the Clydesdale first bred?
2. How much does a Clydesdale weigh?
3. What is distinctive about a Clydesdale's legs?

Text implicit:

1. How tall is a Clydesdale in inches?
2. Why is the feathery hair on the Clydesdale's leg called a sock?
3. What makes the Clydesdale such as good draft horse?

Script implicit (or *scriptal*):

1. What agricultural needs did the Clydesdale meet for farmers?
2. Would a Clydesdale be a good jumper? Why or why not?
3. What other horses have been bred for a specific purpose?

ACTIVITY 93—PARTS OF SPEECH

1. Three homes at Fifth Street and Pine burned. (adj., noun, prep., noun, noun, conj., noun, verb)

2. That dog ran home. (adj., noun, verb, adv.)

3. The red shirts will run in hot water. (adj., adj., noun, verb, verb, prep., adj., noun)

4. Well, I have another run in my sock. (inter., pron., verb, adj., noun, prep., adj., noun)

5. Many children happily played a game. (adj., noun, adv., verb, adj., noun)

6. The play last night was fun. (adj., noun, adj., noun, verb, adj.)

7. Those students have no time for fun and games. (adj., noun, verb, adv., noun, prep., noun, conj., noun)

8. He left his book on the bus yesterday. (pron., verb, adj., noun, prep., adj., noun, adv.)

9. No, the teacher said we must finish our assignment. (interj., adj., noun, verb, pron., verb, verb, adj., noun)

10. Two big events are planned for this year. (adj., adj., noun, verb, verb, prep., adj., noun)

ACTIVITY 94—SYNTAX

Answers will vary.

ACTIVITY 95—COMPOSITION: THE DESCRIPTIVE PARAGRAPH

The ubiquitous spoon is an amazingly versatile utensil. One can eat, stir, skim, dip, mold, scoop, dollop, and make rhythmic music with a spoon. Its long slender handle accounts for its easy maneuverability. Its half-bulbous bowl is responsible for its adaptability. [*The previous two sentences can go in either order.*] The spoon is as precious to a chef as a precision jigsaw is to a master craftsman. Our world would be a different place without the incredible, versatile spoon.[a]

New descriptive paragraphs will vary.

ACTIVITY 96—COMPOSITION: WRITING A DESCRIPTIVE/PERSUASIVE PARAGRAPH

Paragraphs will vary.

ACTIVITY 97—COMPOSITION: WRITING A DESCRIPTIVE/PERSUASIVE PARAGRAPH

Paragraphs will vary.

ACTIVITY 98—COMPOSITION: THE PAINLESS PARAGRAPH

Here is an example of a painless paragraph using the picture of the cowboy from Figure 6:

The Setting Sun
A cloudless sky darkens as a lonesome cowboy surveys the land. His faithful horse waits patiently. The cowboy gently pulls the rein in his hands. The horse raises his head and flutters his tail. Together they watch as the fading sun sinks below the horizon.[b]

[a]Paragraph used with permission of Neuhaus Education Center.
[b]Sentences used with permission of Neuhaus Education Center.

ACTIVITY 99—COMPOSITION: TRANSITION WORDS AND PHRASES

Time and sequence: *first, finally, before*

Emphasis: *obviously, above all, keep in mind*

Change of direction: *yet, otherwise, certainly*

Illustration: *for example, specifically, as an illustration*

Conclusion: *therefore, thus, in summary*

ACTIVITY 100—REASON FOR THE FINAL *e*

Word	Reason for Silent *e*	Derivatives
name	Vowel-consonant-*e*	naming, named, nameless
shave	Vowel-consonant-*e*; base words do not end in *v*	shaving, shaved, shaver
battle	Consonant-*le*	battling, battled, battlement
infringe	Soft *g*	infringing, infringer, infringement
trace	Vowel-consonant-*e* and soft *c*	tracing, traced, traceable

ACTIVITY 101—TERMS FOR ASSESSMENT

1) n, 2) e, 3) k, 4) d, 5) b, 6) m, 7) l, 8) g, 9) o, 10) f, 11) j, 12) i, 13) a, 14) c, 15) h

ACTIVITY 102—TERMS FOR PLANNING OF MULTISENSORY LESSONS AND THE CLASSROOM ENVIRONMENT AND ADOLESCENT LITERACY: OLDER STUDENTS STRUGGLING WITH READING

1) e, 2) d, 3) a, 4) b, 5) f, 6) c

ACTIVITY 103—CREATING AN EDUCATIONAL MEMORIES SAMPLE

Educational memories samples will vary. See Chapter 19 in Birsh (2011) for sample excerpts and further discussion of educational memories.

ACTIVITY 104—SPANISH PHONEMES

English consonant sound **with cognate in Spanish:** /m/ (yes), /s/ (yes), /sh/ (no), /t/ (yes), /d/ (yes), /j/ (no), /zh/ (no), /k/ (yes), /th/ (no) (*Note:* The unvoiced /th/ sound and the /zh/ sound are used in Castilian Spanish.)

Spanish consonant sound **with cognate in English:** /rr/ (no), /b/ (yes), /ñ/ (no), /p/ (yes), /g/ (yes), /f/ (yes), /ch/ (yes), /1/ (yes)

ACTIVITY 105—TERMS FOR EXECUTIVE FUNCTION AND LEARNING STRATEGIES, ADOLESCENT LITERACY, MULTISENSORY MATHEMATICS INSTRUCTION, ASSISTIVE TECHNOLOGY, AND THE LAW

1) f, 2) k, 3) g, 4) j, 5) a, 6) j, 7) l, 8) e, 9) d, 10) m, 11) h, 12) c, 13) i, 14) t, 15) n, 16) u, 17) s, 18) o, 19) p, 20) q, 21) r

ACTIVITY 106—PLANNING 5 DAYS OF LESSONS

Lesson plans will vary. See Figures 15.1, 15.2, 15.3 and15.4 in Birsh and Schedler (2011) for samples of beginning- and intermediate-level plans, respectively.

Activities Coordinated with
Becoming a Professional Reading Teacher: What to Teach, How to Teach, Why It Matters
(Aaron, Joshi, & Quatroche, 2008)

Chapter 3—The Psycholinguistics of Spoken Language
   Activities 7, 8, 9, 10, 11, 12, 13, 14, 15, 17, 18, 19, 20

Chapter 4—The Psycholinguistics of Written Language
   Activities 4, 5, 6, 21, 22, 40, 41

Chapter 5—Development of Spoken and Written Language Skills
   Activities 28, 29, 30, 31

Chapter 6—Developing Basic Literacy Skills
   Activities 16, 23, 24, 25, 26

Chapter 7—Strategies for Developing Decoding, Instant Word Reading, and Spelling Skills
   Activities 16, 33, 34, 35, 36, 37, 38, 39, 42, 43, 44, 45, 46, 47, 48, 49, 50, 51, 52, 53, 54, 55, 56, 57, 58, 59, 60, 61, 62, 63, 64, 65, 66, 67, 68, 69, 70, 71, 72, 73, 74, 75, 99

Chapter 8—Strategies for Developing Vocabulary Knowledge, Comprehension Skills, and Writing Skills
   Activities 76, 77, 78, 79, 80, 81, 82, 83, 84, 85, 86, 87, 88, 89, 90, 91, 92, 93, 94, 95, 96, 97, 98

References

Aaron, P.G., Joshi, R.M., & Quatroche, D. (2008). *Becoming a professional reading teacher: What to teach, how to teach, why it matters.* Baltimore: Paul H. Brookes Publishing Co.

Adams, M.J. (1990). *Beginning to read: Thinking and learning about print.* Cambridge, MA: The MIT Press.

Allen, KA. (with Neuhaus, G.F., & Beckwith, M.C.). (2011). Alphabet knowledge: Letter recognition, naming, and sequencing. In J.R. Birsh (Ed.), *Multisensory teaching of basic language skills* (3rd ed., pp. 145–178). Baltimore: Paul H. Brookes Publishing Co.

Barrutia, R., & Schwegler, A. (1994). *Fonética y fonología españolas* [Spanish phonics and phonology] (2nd ed.). New York: John Wiley & Sons.

Birsh, J.R. (Ed.). (2011). *Multisensory teaching of basic language skills* (3rd ed.). Baltimore: Paul H. Brookes Publishing Co.

Birsh, J.R., & Schedler, J.-F. (2011). Planning multisensory structured language lessons and the classroom environment. In J.R. Birsh (Ed.), *Multisensory teaching of basic language skills* (3rd ed., pp. 459–486). Baltimore: Paul H. Brookes Publishing Co.

Blumenthal, S. (1981). *Educational memories.* Unpublished manuscript.

Blumenthal, S. (2011). Working with high functioning adults with dyslexia and other academic challenges. In J.R. Birsh (Ed.), *Multisensory teaching of basic language skills* (3rd ed., pp. 589–606). Baltimore: Paul H. Brookes Publishing Co.

Brady, S., & Moats, L.C. (1997). *Informed instruction for reading success: Foundations for teacher preparation* (A position paper of The International Dyslexia Association). Baltimore: The International Dyslexia Association.

Carreker, S. (2002). *Scientific spelling.* Bellaire, TX: Neuhaus Education Center.

Carreker, S. (2004). *Developing metacognitive skills.* Bellaire, TX: Neuhaus Education Center.

Carreker, S. (2011a). Teaching reading: Accurate decoding. In J.R. Birsh (Ed.), *Multisensory teaching of basic language skills* (3rd ed., pp. 207–250). Baltimore: Paul H. Brookes Publishing Co.

Carreker, S. (2011b). Teaching spelling. In J.R. Birsh (Ed.), *Multisensory teaching of basic language skills* (3rd ed., pp. 251–292). Baltimore: Paul H. Brookes Publishing Co.

Cox, A.R. (1984). *Structures and techniques: Multisensory teaching of basic written English skills.* Cambridge, MA: Educators Publishing Service.

Cox, A.R. (1992). *Foundations for literacy: Structures and techniques for multisensory teaching of basic written English skills.* Cambridge, MA: Educators Publishing Service.

Cox, A.R., & Hutcheson, L.M. (1988). Syllable division: A prerequisite of dyslexics' literacy. *Annals of Dyslexia, 38,* 226–242.

Farrell, M.L., & Sherman, G. (2011). Multisensory structured language education. In J.R. Birsh (Ed.), *Multisensory teaching of basic language skills* (3rd ed., pp. 25–48). Baltimore: Paul H. Brookes Publishing Co.

Good, R. H., & Kiminski, R. A. (2002). Dynamic indicators of basic early literacy skills (DIBELS). Eugene, OR: Institute for the Development of Education Achievement.

Hanna, P.R., Hanna, J.S., Hodges, R.E., & Rudorf, E.H. (1966). *Phoneme–grapheme correspondences as cues to spelling improvement.* Washington, DC: U.S. Government Printing Office, U.S. Office of Education.

Hennessy, N. (2011). Word learning and vocabulary instruction. In J.R. Birsh (Ed.), *Multisensory teaching of basic language skills* (3rd ed., pp. 321–366). Baltimore: Paul H. Brookes Publishing Co.

Henry, M.K. (1988). Beyond phonics: Integrating decoding and spelling instruction based on word origin and structure. *Annals of Dyslexia, 38,* 259–277.

Henry, M.K. (2010). Unlocking literacy: effective decoding and spelling instruction.

Henry, M.K. (2011). The history and structure of written English. In J.R. Birsh (Ed.), *Multisensory teaching of basic language skills* (3rd ed., pp. 93–112). Baltimore: Paul H. Brookes Publishing Co.

Hochman, J.C. (2011). Composition: Evidence-based instruction In J.R. Birsh (Ed.), *Multisensory teaching of basic language skills* (3rd ed., pp. 407–428). Baltimore: Paul H. Brookes Publishing Co.

Invernizzi, M., Meier, J, & Juel, C. (2002) Phonological awareness screening 1-3 (PALS). Charlottesville: University of Virginia.

Lyon, G.R. (1999). The NICHD research program in reading development, reading disorders, and reading instruction: a summary of research findings. In *Keys to successful learning: A national summit on research in learning disabilities.* New York: National Center for Learning Disabilities.

Marzola, E.S. (2011). Strategies to improve reading comprehension in the multisensory classroom. In J.R. Birsh (Ed.), *Multisensory teaching of basic language skills* (3rd ed., pp. 367–406). Baltimore: Paul H. Brookes Publishing Co.

Merriam Webster's Collegiate™ Dctionary, 11th Edition. © (2011). Springfield, MA: Merriam-Webster, Inc.

Moats, L.C. (1995). *Spelling: Development, disabilities and instruction.* Timonium, MD: York Press.

Moats, L.C. (2010). *Speech to print: Language essentials for teachers.* Baltimore: Paul H. Brookes Publishing Co.

Neuhaus Education Center. (1998). *Basic language skills: concept manual, book two.* Bellaire, TX: Author.

Neuhaus Education Center. (2000). *The colors and shapes of language.* Bellaire, TX: Author.

Nissenbaum, C., & Henley, A. (2011). Learning strategies and study skills: The SkORE System. In J.R. Birsh (Ed.), *Multisensory teaching of basic language skills* (3rd ed., pp. 551–558). Baltimore: Paul H. Brookes Publishing Co.

Pearson, P.D., & Johnson, D.D. (1978). *Teaching reading comprehension.* Austin, TX: Holt, Rinehart & Winston.

Piastra, S.B., Connor, C.M., Fishman, B.J., & Morrison, F. J. (2009). Teachers' knowledge of literary concepts, classroom practices, and student reading growth. *Scientific Studies of Reading, 13*(3), 224–248.

Read, C. (1971). Pre-school children's knowledge of English phonology. *Harvard Educational Review, 41,* 1–34.

Robinson, E.P. (1946). *Effective study.* New York: HarperCollins.

Rumsey, J.M. (1996). Neuroimaging in developmental dyslexia: a review and conceptualization. In G.R. Lyon & J.M. Rumsey (Eds.), *Neuroimaging: A window to the neurological foundation of learning and behavior in children* (pp. 57–77).

Stanback, M.L. (1992). Analysis of frequency-based vocabulary of 17,602 words. *Annals of Dyslexia, 42,* 196–221.

Steere, A., Peck, C.Z., & Kahn, L. (1984). *Solving language difficulties: Remedial routines.* Cambridge, MA: Educators Publishing Service.

Torgesen, J.K. (1997). The prevention and remediation of reading disabilities: Evaluating what we know from research. *Journal of Academic Language Therapy, 1,* 11–47.

University of Texas System and Texas Education Agency. (2006). *Texas primary reading inventory.* Austin, TX: Authors.

Wilson, B.A. (2011). Instruction for older students with a word-level reading disability. In J.R. Birsh (Ed.), *Multisensory teaching of basic language skills* (3rd ed., pp. 489–518). Baltimore: Paul H. Brookes Publishing Co.

Wolf, B.J. (2011). Teaching handwriting. In J.R. Birsh (Ed.), *Multisensory teaching of basic language skills* (3rd ed., pp. 179–206). Baltimore: Paul H. Brookes Publishing Co.